W9-CER-696

PATRICE BOËLY

New York • London • Toronto • Sydney

All inquiries should be addressed to:
Barron's Educational Series, Inc.
250 Wireless Boulevard
Hauppauge, New York 11788

Library of Congress Catalog Card No. 87-31675
International Standard Book No. 0-8120-5838-0

Library of Congress Cataloging in Publication Data

Boëly, Patrice.
The joy of seafood/Patrice Boëly.
p. cm.
Includes Index.
ISBN 0-8120-5838-0
1. Cookery (Fish) I. Title 2. Cookery (Seafood)
TX747.B56 1988
641.6'92—dc19 87-31675
CIP

PRINTED IN THE UNITED STATES OF AMERICA
890 9770 987654321

Credits

Cover and book design: Milton Glaser, Inc.
Color photographs: Matthew Klein
Food Styling: Rick Ellis
Photo Styling: Linda Cheverton

Patricia Connell, Editor

Photo Credits

Villeroy and Boch, fine porcelain and china, available at fine stores everywhere.

Gordon Foster, handthrown porcelain dishes, 1322 Third Avenue, New York, NY. 10021

Georg Jensen, sterling silver flatware from Royal Copenhagen, 683 Madison Avenue, New York, NY. 10021

Simon Pearce, handthrown casseroles and crystals, 385 Bleeker Street, New York, NY. 10012

Table of Contents

Foreword

by Roger Vergé

In writing this book, Patrice Boëly generously shares with you the secrets and expertise mastered during a lifetime of cooking. His mastery of fish cookery was the joy of the food cognoscenti during his years at the Moulin de Mougins in France. Today, at the Polo Restaurant in New York, he continues to gain the recognition he so richly deserves.

This book is a testament to the love that Chef Boëly holds for his profession. His sincerity and the easy manner in which he gives his recipes will enable the aspiring amateur, as well as the professional chef, to reproduce them. If by chance a recipe is modified, then it will bear the cook's signature.

As my dear friend Danny Kaye often said, "One needs to be generous to be a cook." He was so right because cooking is a means of expressing one's feelings, communicating, and sharing. Who could be more sincere than the chef who shares his recipes, advice, tips, ideas, and love of his calling?

The mark of the true chef: To share the joys of the palate as the painter does with his painting and the musician does through his music.

Introduction

In this book I have tried to bring to the reader the essence of my cooking, which comes from a background of diverse climates and cultures. They include Corsica, my birthplace; Denmark, where I worked for many years; Provence, namely the Michelin three-star Moulin de Mougins; and now, America.

When I was a child, my grandfather, an avid fisherman, taught me everything he knew about fishing—a considerable store of knowledge. He perfected his skills during World War II when food was scarce and there were many mouths to feed. One of them was a downed Canadian pilot, hidden under the floor during the German occupation.

I enjoy cooking fish because it is a game, a constant challenge. With other foods, timing can be more or less relaxed. But timing is all-important in cooking fish; a few seconds over and it is too late. You've overcooked it. The taste is gone; the texture is cottony.

In this book, I hope to help you rid yourself of the fear of cooking fish and learn to love the challenge as I do.

I wish to express my gratitude to Gloria Zimmerman for her invaluable help in making this book possible.

Patrice Boëly

Equipment

As far as pots and pans are concerned, there are no special requirements other than what is already available in your kitchen. I have made suggestions along with each technique. A few general recommendations follow:

- Good heavy-bottomed skillets in several sizes (no coated nonstick pans)
- A food processor is desirable
- Scissors for cutting through shells, gills, fins and tails
- A fish poacher is very helpful. The rack inside helps keep the fish intact as it is removed from the poaching liquid.
- Trussing needles—for sewing fish after stuffing
- Pastry bag with a plain tip—for stuffing fish
- Mallet—for breaking crabs
- Nutcracker—for cracking lobster claws
- Fish scaler or scallop shell for scaling fish
- Mortar and pestle—in case you don't have a food processor.

My Cooking Secrets

1 Find a good, reliable fishmonger—which means a market that's busy and that doesn't smell fishy. The eyes of the fish should be clear, and the gills should be red and not sticky. (Sometimes dye is added to the gills, but the test for stickiness will still show whether the fish is fresh.) The scales and skin should be shiny and the meat firm. Fillets should be firm and, again, not sticky. Don't be ashamed to ask to smell the fish—it should be odorless.

Storage is of vital importance. When dealing with fish just purchased, it's best to cook it as soon as possible, since it will probably have been caught several days earlier. Fish should be eviscerated as quickly as possible because uneviscerated fish deteriorates very rapidly. If the fish must be held for a day after purchase, first wash and dry it. Then fill a shallow pan or glass dish with ice, cover the ice with plastic wrap and lay the fish on top. Cover with a damp towel and, of course, refrigerate. This method applies to whole fish, fillets and steaks alike.

2 To remove the skin of Dover sole and grey sole (only these two varieties): dip the tail, just to where the skin begins, into very hot water for five seconds. The skin will pull off both sides with no effort.

3 It's best to slightly undercook fish. Stop cooking while preparing sauce. After removing it from heat, set the fish aside, covered with foil. The fish will continue to cook from retained heat.

4 Oysters or clams that are to be cooked (not eaten raw) are easily opened by placing them in a 350°F oven for 1 to 1½ minutes; they will open slightly and can be pried open with a knife.

5 Skate, turbot and brill—After braising or poaching, place on a cold plate, gray side down. Remove the white skin with a knife, then lift the fish from the plate and the gray skin will stay behind on the plate. Trout and pike—The same method applies—after braising only.

6 Whole fish—To test for doneness, insert a sharp knife through the fleshiest part where the head meets the body. If the meat sticks to the bone or there is still a trace of pinkness, the fish is not completely cooked.

7 Salmon and cod steaks (with center bone)—If the bone comes away easily with just a little resistance, the fish is ready. If it comes away too easily, it is overcooked.

8 To serve a fish steak without the skin, after it is cooked pierce the skin with a fork and turn it like a key; the skin will unwind.

9 For a beautiful presentation of lobster, place it on a piece of wood, shell side up, and tie the lobster to the board with string. Cook it this way and it will not curl. Remove the tail meat, slice into medallions and place them atop the shell. Remember to remove the strings before serving.

Cooking Techniques

Baking

Because this is cooking with dry heat, the oven temperature and time should be carefully monitored. Electric ovens tend to maintain temperatures more accurately than gas ovens.

Braising

This term refers to cooking in liquid that does not cover the food. A relatively small amount of liquid remains to be used for making sauce.

Deep-frying

In this technique, the fish is totally submerged in a large quantity of cooking oil, preferably peanut, corn or soy. In order to maintain the oil at the proper temperature, it is advisable to cook no more than 1/2 pound of fish at one time in about 4 cups of oil. A deep-frying thermometer or electric wok or electric deep fryer will help in maintaining the proper temperature.

For small quantities, it is more economical to use a small saucepan.

Grilling or Barbecuing

If grilling with charcoal, allow for half an hour to preheat the grill. The briquets or charcoal should be white before placing fish on the grill. A gas grill requires about 10 minutes of preheating. The racks and the fish should be oiled before placing the fish on the grill.

Hickory chips, mesquite or other wood chips add a special flavor. First soak the chips in water for half an hour. Tossing fresh herbs, such as rosemary and thyme, onto the charcoal is another way to add flavor and aroma.

For grilling whole fish, a hinged fish-shaped rack makes cooking and turning much easier. For fillets, a hamburger-type hinged grill is a useful addition to the *batterie de cuisine.*

Marinating

Marinating is used to tenderize and to give flavor before cooking.

Oven broiling

The heat source is above the food rather than below as it is on the barbecue grill. Be sure to preheat the broiler well so that the fish sears quickly.

Poaching

The fish is cooked in liquid to cover. Place the fish in cold or room-temperature liquid, and then bring to the simmering point. It must never be allowed to boil. The simmering process allows the vegetables, herbs and wine to infuse the fish with their flavors.

If fish is to be served cold, it should be refrigerated overnight in the court bouillon. This keeps the fish moist, and the flavor is enhanced as it sits in the broth.

The best piece of equipment for this method of cooking is a fish poacher with a rack that can be lowered and raised, facilitating removal of a whole fish without breaking. In the absence of a fish poacher, the fish can be wrapped in cheesecloth to keep its shape and to facilitate its removal from the pot. A nonaluminum pan is best, because poaching liquid very often contains wine—which will blacken an aluminum pot and discolor the fish.

Raw fish

Must be very, very fresh. A word of caution—you must know your fishmonger before you dare use raw fish.

Sautéing

Sautéing is done either in olive oil, so typical of the cooking of the south of France, or in butter. A small amount of oil or butter is heated in a skillet; the fat should be hot but not smoking before adding the food. If it is too hot, the color will be off, flavor will change for the worse and the food will not be easily digestible.

Steaming

A method of cooking with wet heat. The food never comes in direct contact with liquid; it is cooked by freely circulating steam.

A steamer consists of a pot to contain liquid, a perforated rack that fits into the top of the pot, and a lid. Water or stock is brought to a boil in the pot and the food is placed either directly on the perforated rack or on a plate resting on it. There must be at least one inch between the edge of the plate and the side of the pot to allow the wet steam to circulate.

A steamer can be improvised with any large pot; a rack or any empty tuna fish can, opened at both ends, can serve to hold the plate of food.

Conversion Tables

The cup and spoon measures given in the book are U.S. Customary (cup = 235 mL; 1 tablespoon = 15 mL). Use these tables when working with British Imperial or Metric kitchen utensils.

LIQUID MEASURES

The Imperial pint is larger than the U.S. pint; therefore note the following when measuring liquid ingredients.

U.S.		
1 cup	=	8 fluid ounces
1/2 cup	=	4 fluid ounces
1 tablespoon	=	3/4 fluid ounce

Imperial		
1 cup	=	10 fluid ounces
1/2 cup	=	5 fluid ounces
1 tablespoon	=	1 fluid ounce

U.S. Measure	*Metric**	*Imperial**
1 quart (4 cups)	950 mL	1 1/2 pints + 4 tablespoons
1 pint (2 cups)	450 mL	3/4 pint
1 cup	236 mL	1/4 pint + 6 tablespoons
1 tablespoon	15 mL	1 + tablespoon
1 teaspoon	5 mL	1 teaspoon

**Note that exact quantities are not always given. Differences are more crucial when dealing with larger quantities. For teaspoon and tablespoon measures, simply use scant or generous quantities; or for more accurate conversions, rely upon metric.*

SOLID MEASURES

Outside the U.S., cooks measure more items by weight. Here are approximate equivalents for basic items in this book.*

	U.S. Customary	*Metric*	*Imperial*
Beans (dried, raw)	1 cup	225g	8 ounces
Butter	1 cup	225g	8 ounces
	1/2 cup	115g	4 ounces
	1/4 cup	60g	2 ounces
	1 tablespoon	15g	1/2 ounce
Cheese (grated)	1 cup	115g	4 ounces
Coconut (shredded)	1/2 cup	60g	2 ounces
Fruit (chopped)	1 cup	225g	8 ounces
Herbs (chopped)	1/4 cup	7g	1/4 ounce
Mushrooms (chopped)	1 cup	70g	2 1/2 ounces
Nut Meats (chopped)	1 cup	115g	4 ounces
Pasta (dried, raw)	1 cup	225g	8 ounces
Peas (shelled)	1 cup	225g	8 ounces
Raisins (and other dried fruits)	1 cup	175g	6 ounces
Rice (uncooked)	1 cup	225g	8 ounces
(cooked)	3 cups	225g	8 ounces
Spinach (cooked)	1/2 cup	285g	10 ounces
Vegetables (chopped raw: onion, celery)	1 cup	115g	4 ounces

**To avoid awkward measurements, some conversions are not exact.*

DRY MEASURES

The following items are measured by weight outside of the U.S. These items are variable, especially the flour, depending on individual variety of flour and moisture. American cup measurements on following items are loosely packed; flour is measured directly from package (presifted).

	U.S. Customary	*Metric*	*Imperial*
Flour (all-purpose)	1 cup	150g	5 ounces
	1/2 cup	70g	2 1/2 ounces
Cornmeal	1 cup	175g	6 ounces
Sugar (granulated)	1 cup	190g	6 1/2 ounces
	1/2 cup	85g	3 ounces
	1/4 cup	40g	1 3/4 ounces
(powdered)	1 cup	80g	2 2/3 ounces
	1/2 cup	40g	1 1/3 ounces
	1/4 cup	20g	3/4 ounce
(brown)	1 cup	160g	5 1/3 ounces
	1/2 cup	80g	2 2/3 ounces
	1/4 cup	40g	1 1/3 ounces

OVEN TEMPERATURES

Gas Mark	1/4	2	4	6	8
Fahrenheit	225°	300°	350°	400°	450°
Celsius	110°	150°	180°	200°	230°

Guide to Seafood

Notes on Fish

Black Bass

Native to North America, this is the freshwater counterpart of sea bass. Size varies greatly. The fish has a thick body and large scales; the meat is firm, white and lean, with few bones. The flavor resembles trout, which can be substituted.

Bluefish

Abundant in the Gulf of Mexico and along the East Coast as far north as Canada, traveling in schools from spring to fall. A favorite of sport fishermen because it is a ferocious fighter when hooked. Meat has a high fat content and a strong, rich taste. Like all oily fish, it deteriorates quickly so should be perfectly fresh. Commonly 25 to 30 inches long, ranging to over 40.

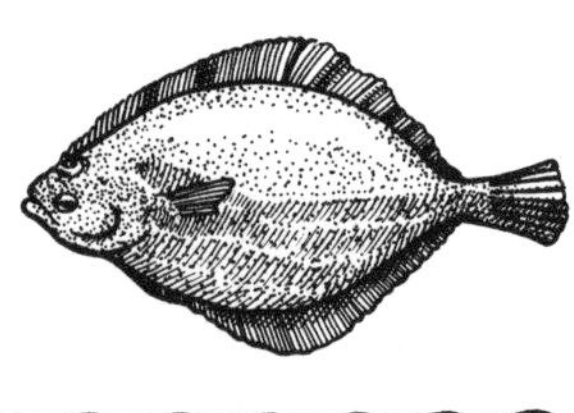

Brill

Also called Petrale sole. A flatfish, common length about 1 foot; see *Flatfish.*

Carp

A freshwater fish found in rivers, lakes and ponds. River-grown carp are preferred, as the others can have a slightly muddy taste (this is least pronounced in cold weather, so the fish is considered to be at its best from October to March). Originally an Asian species, carp was introduced to this continent in the mid-19th century. It can grow to great size, but average market weight is 2 to 7 pounds. Low to moderate in fat content, the fish is highly favored by the Chinese and Central European cooks.

Opposite: Shrimp with Chive and Cinnamon Sauce (page 141).
Page following: Terrine of Black Bass and Asparagus (page 150).

Catfish

A freshwater type, available all year and ranging from 1 to 50 pounds. Most catfish is aquacultured, but it is also caught in lakes and rivers. The flesh is light and delicately flavored but relatively high in fat. The fish is usually sold whole, skinned and dressed; it is occasionally found in the form of steaks and fillets. Catfish has a tough skin that must be removed before cooking.

Char

Related to brook trout, but some char grow in fresh and others in salt water. The delicate flesh may be white or pink. Substitute salmon trout.

Clam

Harvested from sand in the shallows with a rake or tongs. Known all over the world in many varieties, but overall divided into two types: the soft-shell (or steamer) clam and the hardshell. Found in the Atlantic, the steamer clam buries itself and has a long siphon ("neck") extending up to the sand's surface. This siphon gives away the clam's hiding place at low tide. Among the hard-shelled types (from both the Atlantic and the Pacific) are littlenecks, the slightly larger cherrystones, and chowder clams, the largest of all.

Cod

A lean, firm, white-fleshed fish harvested chiefly from the North Atlantic. The name includes a number of species of great importance as food fish. In the U.S., cod up to 3 pounds and 20 inches long are known as scrod; larger specimens range up to 30 inches or more.

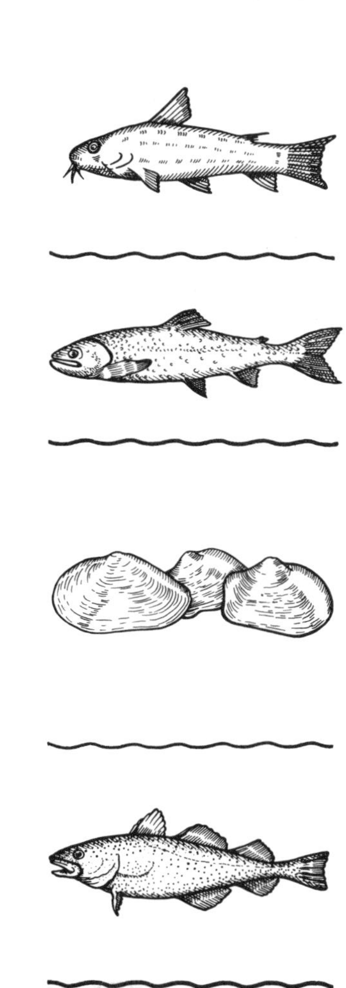

Opposite: Flounder with Tomatoes and Sweet Garlic Sauce (page 68).
Page preceding: Smoked Salmon Trout with Spinach in Puff Pastry (page 153).

Crab

The most abundant type, the Atlantic blue crab, is harvested chiefly from shallow water in Chesapeake Bay but ranges from Delaware Bay to the Gulf of Mexico. It is actually brownish green or dark green, with blue-tinted claws. Maximum body width is over 20 inches. The species' scientific name is *Callinectes* ("beautiful swimmer") *sapidus* ("savory"). Soft-shell crabs are blue crabs that have just shed their hard shells. Since they remain soft for only a day or so, they are caught in advance and kept in special enclosures until they moult. A crab typically sheds its shell about 20 times before reaching full size. Summer is the peak season for Chesapeake soft-shell crabs.

Crayfish

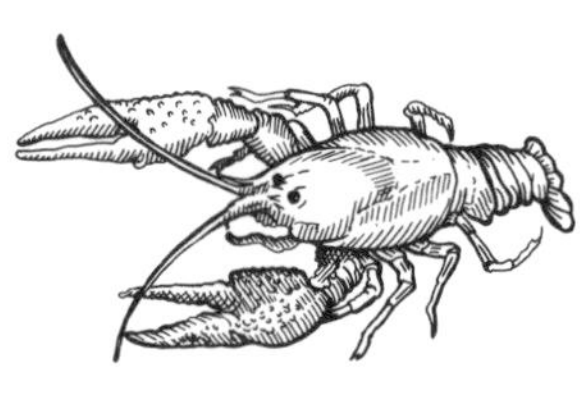

A freshwater lobster, also called crawfish. More easily found in the West and South than on the East Coast. Collected from still or slow-moving water 1 to 10 feet deep; also cultivated in freshwater ponds. Like lobster, crayfish turns scarlet when cooked. Most of the meat is in the tail, but other parts can be used for making stocks and sauces.

Dogfish

A type of shark, typically weighing 12 to 18 pounds; sold in steaks and chunks. Like other shark varieties, it has lean, firm, meaty flesh resembling swordfish. Because shark has only one "bone"—a long, cartilaginous spinal column—the meat is essentially boneless.

Eel

The common eel is born in the Sargasso Sea south of Bermuda, migrates to a European or North American lake or river (where it spends most of its life, and where it is usually caught), and returns to the sea to spawn and die. It is caught at all seasons but winter eels are thought to taste best. The American species, maximum 25 inches long, ranges from Newfoundland to the West Indies. The meat is rich and oily. When possible, buy live eels straight out of a tank. They should weigh about 1½ pounds, smaller ones have too much waste and larger ones can be too fatty.

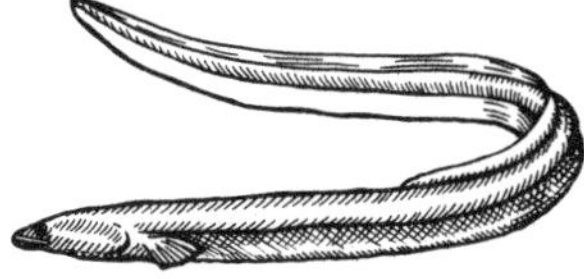

Flatfish

A seabed-dwelling family that includes brill, flounder, halibut, plaice, sand dab, sole and turbot (the latter two found only in European waters). All have thin, flat bodies and white flesh, are easy to fillet, and—a distinctive characteristic of flatfish—both eyes are on one side of the head. One type can generally be substituted for another.

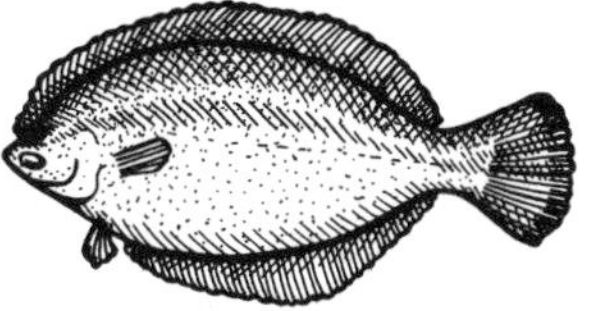

Flounder

A European and American flatfish, maximum length about 20 inches; see *Flatfish.* Though they are interchangeable, flounder is somewhat coarser, thinner and more fragile than sole. *Grey sole* and *Lemon sole* are actually types of flounder.

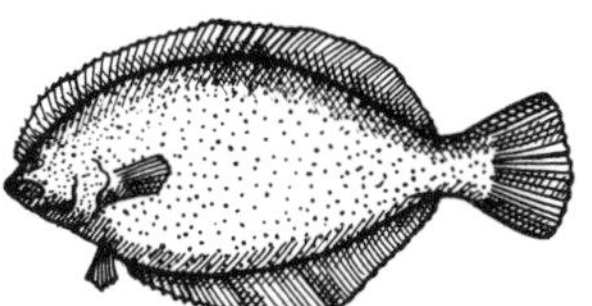

Grey Sole—See *Sole.*

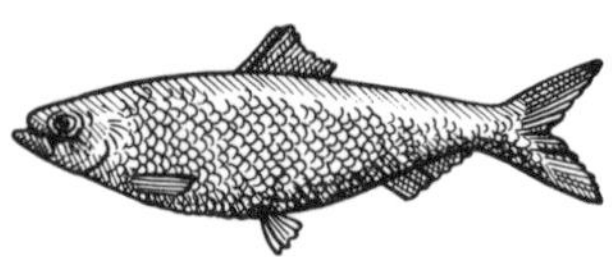

Grouper

Found in the Atlantic and warmer parts of the Mediterranean; where warm currents are present, can be caught as far north as Cape Hatteras. Large (up to 3-foot) grouper are cut into steaks; smaller ones are eaten whole or filleted. The flesh is so similar to sea bass that it is sometimes sold under that name.

Haddock

A smaller member of the cod family, typically 16 to 24 inches long and 2 to 6 pounds. The flesh is mild, white and slightly chewy. Fished as far south as New England. *Finnan haddie,* which originated in Scotland, is smoked haddock.

Halibut

By far the largest of the flatfish, occasionally up to 10 feet and 650 pounds. Caught in deep, cold Atlantic and Pacific waters; strictly an American species. The lean, snowy white flesh may be filleted or cut into steaks. See *Flatfish.*

Herring

Once the most plentiful of fish, distributed across the North Atlantic as far south as Chesapeake Bay, the herring has been decimated by overfishing. Firm and relatively fatty, it is less often eaten fresh than salted, pickled, smoked or canned. *Kippers* are herring that have been brined and cold smoked; other smoked fish can be substituted.

John Dory

Also called St.-Pierre or St. Peter's fish. Found on the American side of the Atlantic but not fished commercially in this country. In France, it is one of the classic ingredients of bouillabaisse. John Dory is an ugly fish with a large, spiny head, but it produces excellent white fillets; substitute sole, flounder or porgy.

Kipper—See *Herring.*

Langoustine

A miniature version of lobster, usually sold cooked, shelled and frozen. Body reaches 10 inches in length, and orange color of shell does not change with cooking. Also called Norway lobster and Dublin Bay prawn. Found in sea-bottom mud from Iceland to the Mediterranean. Langoustines are the true Italian *scampi* (singular *scampo*), a word that in this country is misapplied to shrimp.

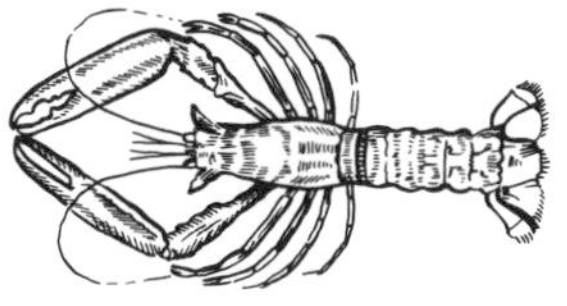

Lemon Sole—See *Sole.*

Lobster

The largest crustacean, found in salt water. Has smooth shell and two large claws of unequal size. Grows very slowly; at five years of age lobster is only 10 to 11 inches long. Because of the labor involved in catching lobsters, they are among the most expensive of seafood. Caught in both European and East Coast waters; the Canadian catch is twice the size of the American. Size varies greatly, from 12- to 16-ounce "chicks" to giants many times this weight. *Spiny lobster,* the West Coast and Gulf variety, has coarser-textured meat and does not have large claws. Resembling a marine crayfish, it is the source of rock lobster tails.

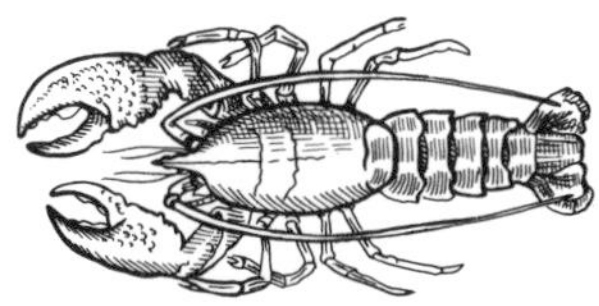

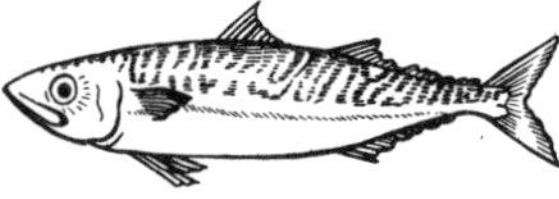

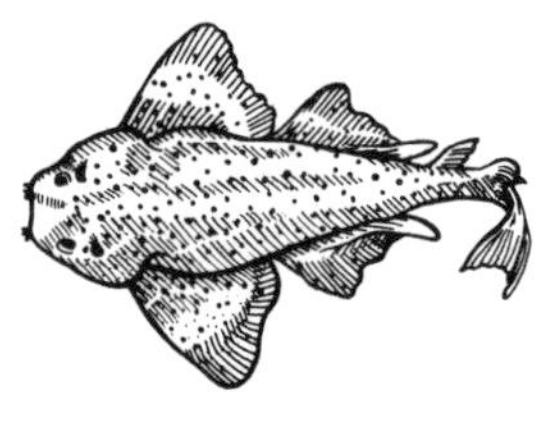

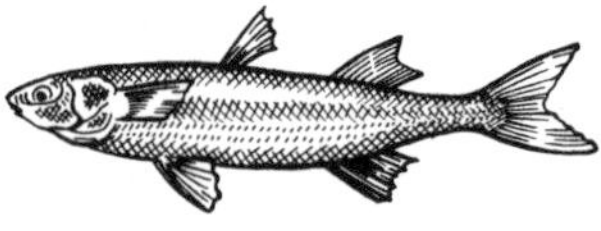

Mackerel

A dark, oily, assertive flavored fish that, like others of the type, deteriorates quickly once caught. A good candidate for acid marinades. Same family as tuna; both fish migrate great distances and are found around the world. Fish is long and slender; typical market length is 12 to 14 inches.

Monkfish

Also called gooseflesh or anglerfish. A bizarrely ugly species, up to 6 feet in length, whose tail is the only edible part. Removing the backbone leaves two perfect boneless fillets of lean white meat so firm that it is often compared to lobster.

Mullet

A relatively small fish found in both fresh and salt water; favored in the American South. The meat is firm, flaky and moderate to high in fat. An important food fish from earliest times, it was already cultivated in ancient Egypt and is now farmed in Hawaii and the Philippines. Most domestic mullet is from Florida; it is in season in fall and winter. The fish are sold whole or dressed. White-fleshed and finely textured, *Red mullet* (called goatfish in this country and *rouget* in France) is popular in the Mediterranean.

Mussel

A familiar, relatively inexpensive mollusk, usually with 2- to $2^{1}/_{2}$-inch blue-black shell. Found in all the oceans of the world and also cultivated; the best are taken from colder waters. Before cooking the mussel must be scrubbed clean and debearded, which means pulling away the tuft of fibers that anchors the animal to its perch. Always discard any mussels that do not open after cooking; this indicates that they were dead, and possibly spoiled.

Octopus

A cephalopod, which means "head-footed," indicating that the tentacles sprout directly from the head. Size varies widely, commonly between 16 and 40 inches. Sold fresh in ethnic markets but more commonly frozen. Octopus found in American markets is almost always from Pacific waters.

Oyster

A bivalve mollusk relished from earliest times, oysters grow in shallow coastal waters all over the world; they are also cultivated. During and after spawning in late spring the flesh tends to be thin and watery—thus the taboo against eating oysters in "non-R" months (it is not because they are unsafe during those months). There are various types, of which the commonest in the U.S. is the gray, rough-shelled Eastern oyster up to $6^{1}/_{2}$ inches in length. Some oysters are named for the specific locale where they are harvested—Blue Point (Long Island), Belon (originally from Brittany, but now successfully cultivated in Maine). Market supply usually dictates the cook's choice; Atlantic oysters are in season from September to May, while Pacific varieties are sold year round.

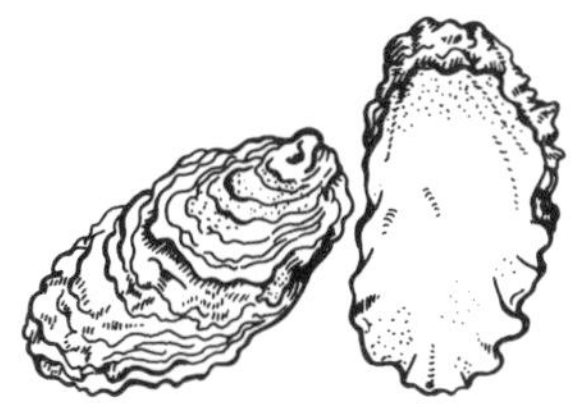

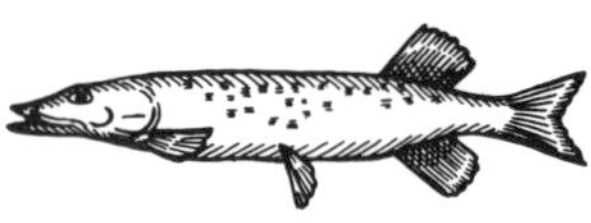

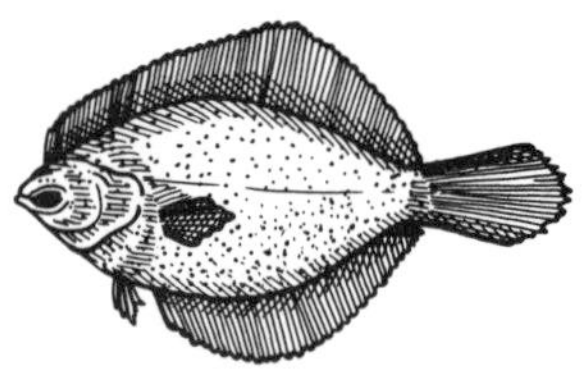

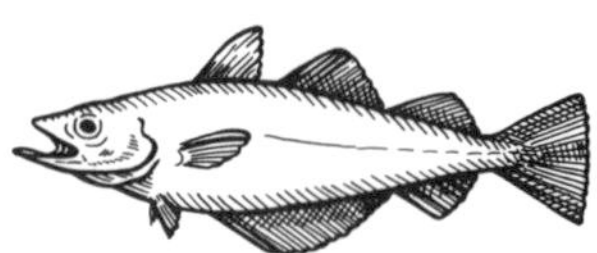

Perch

A long fish with pointed nose and sharp teeth; reaches about 4 pounds. Principally a game fish, found in fresh or low-salinity salt water; rarely reaches the commercial market. Considered by the French among the best of freshwater types; the firm, lean flesh has a delicate texture and absorbent quality that make it very good with sauces.

Pike

A freshwater fish with long body, pugnacious jaw and many strong teeth. The firm white flesh is lean and sweet. Typical weight is 3 to 4 pounds.

Plaice

Usually about 20 inches long, plaice is popular and abundant in Europe; see *Flatfish.* It it found along both European and American coasts, in this country as far south as Rhode Island. Also called *Sand dab* or fluke.

Pollack

A member of the cod family, caught in rocky coastal waters over a very large area of the Atlantic. In season during the winter; typical specimens are 16 to 20 inches long. Cod or haddock may be substituted.

Pompano

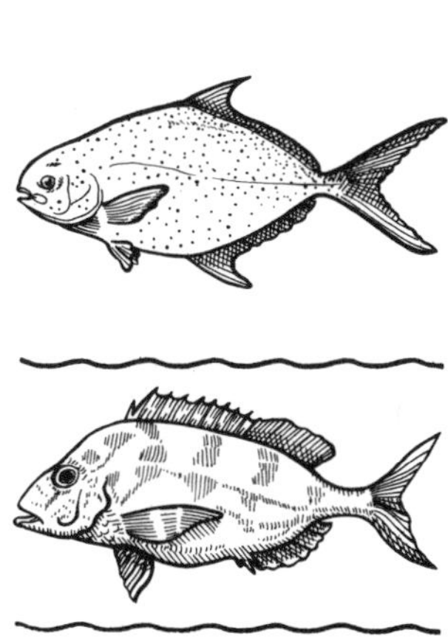

Caught as far north as Chesapeake Bay, this is considered by many to be the best fish in the South Atlantic and Gulf of Mexico; it is correspondingly expensive. A handsome round fish with blue-green scales shading to silver at the belly, it grows to about 18 inches and 1½ to 3 pounds. The flesh is firm, well-flavored and slightly fatty.

Porgy

Also known as sea bream or scup. Usually 1½ to 2 pounds, it is generally eaten whole, not filleted. Found in the Atlantic from South Carolina to Maine. Flesh is lean, white and flavorful.

Prawn—Name used outside the U.S. for large shrimp; see *Shrimp.*

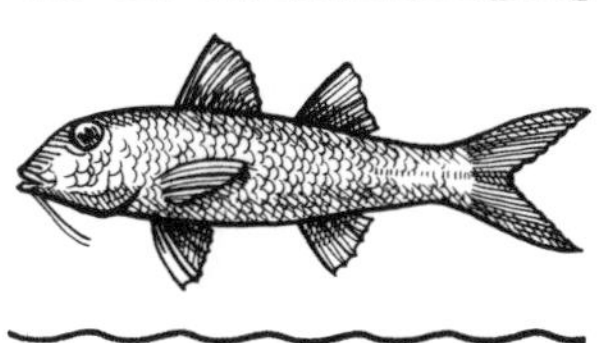

Red mullet—See *Mullet.*

Red Snapper—See *Snapper.*

Salmon

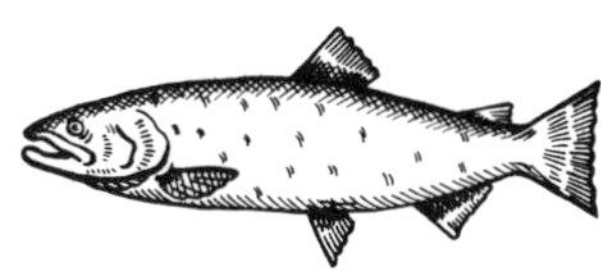

The salmon's life cycle is the inverse of the eel's: The fish is born in a river, spends its adult life at sea, and returns to the river to spawn or be caught. The Atlantic salmon lives for two or three spawning seasons, the Pacific type for only one. Pacific subtypes include coho, Chinook, chum and red sockeye. When fully grown, salmon may be 32 to 36 inches long and weigh 25 pounds or more. The flesh is firm, compact and moderate to high in fat. Its orange color is a result of the fish's diet of crustaceans. Because it is so flavorful, salmon is usually simply prepared.

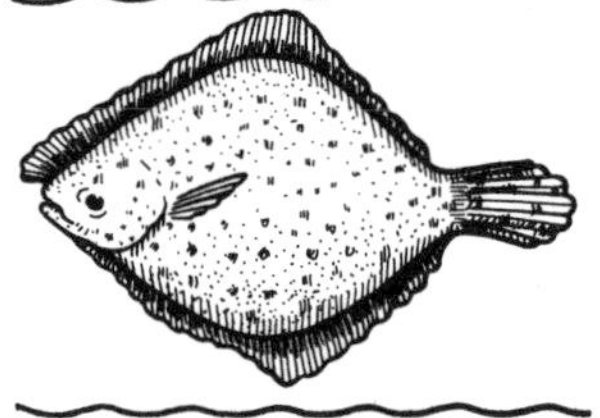

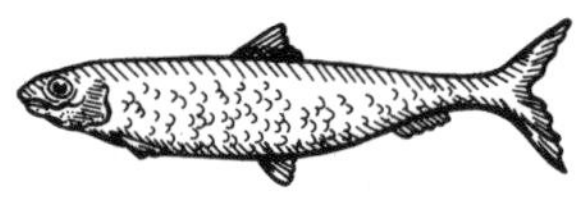

Salmon trout

A pink-fleshed member of the trout family. There are both fresh- and salt-water types. As with salmon, the flesh is colored by pigments in the crustaceans that the fish eats. Size varies widely, with saltwater varieties larger than freshwater ones. Substitute salmon.

Sand dab

An American variety of the European plaice; see *Flatfish*. Maximum length about 2 feet. Often confused with other flatfish such as flounder and sole.

Sardine

An immature pilchard or herring. Maximum length of the adult is about 10 inches. Fished in a wide range from the Mediterranean to the North Atlantic. Flesh is high in fat and has a soft, fine texture. Since the fish deteriorates quickly after it is caught, it is often salted or canned in oil. Substitute young fresh herring.

Scallop

A bivalve mollusk named for its scalloped shell, but almost always sold shelled. Common on both American coasts. Unlike clams and oysters, the scallop propels itself along the ocean floor by rapidly opening and closing its shell. This motion disproportionately develops the round muscle that acts as the hinge. It is this muscle that is the edible part of the animal. *Sea scallops* and *bay scallops* are both common in the market. The sea scallop is much the larger of the two, with a muscle up to 2 inches in diameter; the sweeter, tenderer bay scallop is a miniature version about 1/2 inch across.

Sea bass

A very good and versatile white-fleshed fish found in both the Atlantic and the Pacific; called rockfish on the West Coast. Popular in Chinese and Italian cooking. Depending on the type, can grow to hundreds of pounds. Flesh is thick, firm and moist, with moderate fat. Substitute grouper.

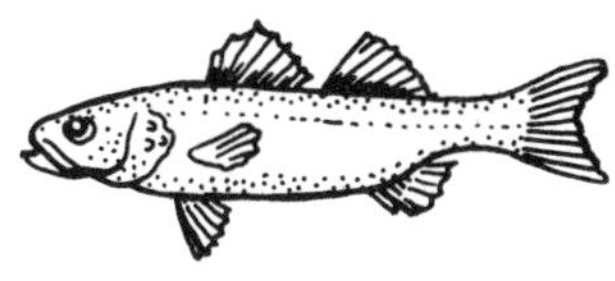

Sea urchin

A ball-shaped creature, about 3 inches in diameter, covered with green spines and found all over the world on rocks at low tide. The edible part is the orange "roe," actually the ovaries.

Shad

Available only before June 1, when spawning begins and the fish's eating quality declines. Extensive range along both Atlantic and Pacific coasts. Like salmon, shad are born in rivers, migrate to sea, and return to the river after several years to spawn or be caught. Both the roe and the fatty flesh are great delicacies, but because the fish is filled with tiny bones it is usually filleted. Freshly caught shad must be iced for two or three days to firm the flesh, or it will fall apart during boning.

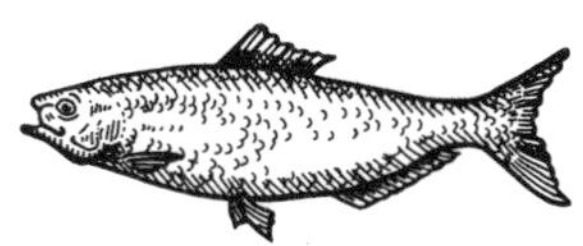

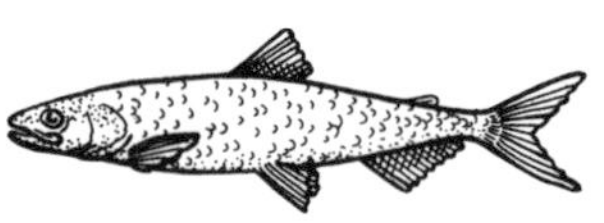

Shrimp

Probably the most popular crustacean in this country, shrimp vary widely in size from about 10 to 35 per pound (tiny Alaskan shrimp up to 160 per pound). Largest domestic harvest is from the Carolinas, Florida, the Gulf of Mexico and the Pacific Coast from Mexico to Alaska. Only the tail is eaten, but the other parts can be used to flavor stocks and sauces. The dark line running just under the surface of the tail meat is the gut, usually called the "vein"; it should be removed from all but the smallest shrimp before cooking.

Skate

A non-bony, flat, scaleless deepwater fish of the ray family; the edible portion is the wide, thin wing. Skate flesh is low in fat and has such fine texture and flavor, owing largely to the fish's consumption of mollusks, that it is sometimes used as a substitute for scallop. Can reach 6 feet in length.

Smelt

From Anglo-Saxon word *smoelt,* meaning smooth and shining. A small (about 8-inch), silvery species found in both salt and fresh water, extensively fished commercially. Smelt have an unusual, somewhat vegetable-like aroma and flavor. The flesh is sweet and tender.

Snapper

The fish in this large and important family differ very widely in size, so they lend themselves to various preparations. *Red snapper,* the most popular variety, is found in warmer parts of the Atlantic and Pacific. It is especially popular in Mexican and Caribbean cuisines. Snapper can grow to 35 pounds, but market size is generally $1\frac{1}{2}$ to 6 pounds. The flesh is firm and low in fat.

Sole

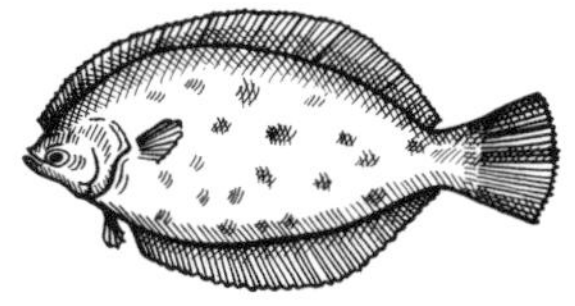

An exceptionally delicious and easily filleted fish, but the only true sole available in this country are imported from England and France. Other flatfish can be substituted (see *Flatfish*). Highly esteemed *Grey sole* is not actually a sole but a witch flounder. *Lemon sole* (really a winter flounder, so called because in winter it comes closer to shore in search of warmer water) is an especially thick, meaty flatfish.

Squid

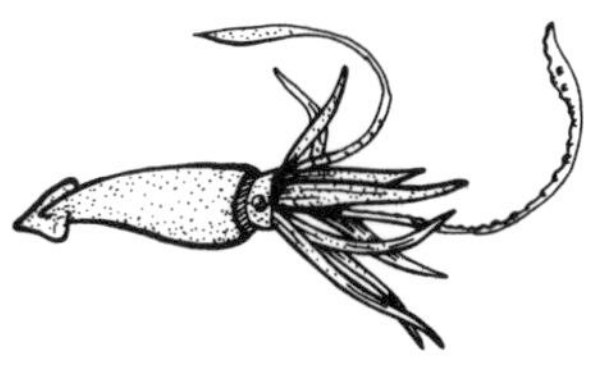

A widely distributed cephalopod (see *Octopus*), which must be cooked either very briefly or long and slowly to prevent toughening. Especially popular in Mediterranean and Oriental cuisines; in this country, caught along the East and Gulf Coasts and in the Monterey Bay area. The body is a tapered tube with triangular fins. No matter what cooking method is used, the innards, the transparent "quill" and the tough "beak" must be removed beforehand; also discard the fins and purplish skin. Typical market size is 6 to 12 inches; a 6-inch squid weighs about 4 ounces. Those under 10 ounces are the most tender.

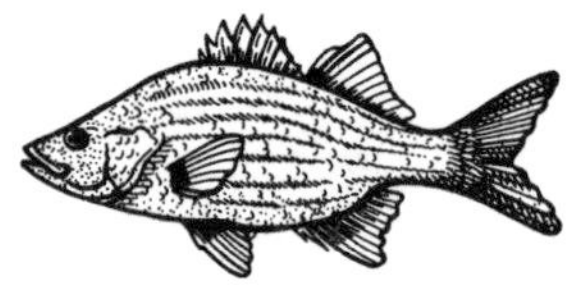

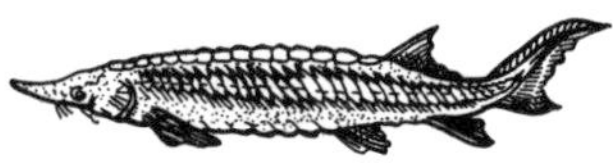

Striped bass

Related to sea bass; an inshore species that is a great favorite of game fishermen from eastern Canada to the Gulf of Mexico, as well as along the Pacific coast. The fish migrates up rivers to spawn. Its white, slighly fatty flesh lends itself to numerous preparation methods. Usual market size is 10 to 18 inches, but the fish can be up to 8 or 10 pounds.

Sturgeon

Once an extremely abundant fish, sturgeon is now in scarce supply, having been harvested for both caviar and meat for centuries. It is an extremely ancient species with a unique skeletal structure that is partly bony, partly cartilaginous. Equally unusual in flavor, the dense, high-fat pink flesh is often compared to veal. Sturgeon is the world's largest freshwater fish, sometimes growing to 12 feet or more.

Swordfish

A large (6-foot or more), wide-ranging species with a distinctive flat, sharp-pointed sword. The swordfish has firm, compact, slightly oily flesh that is exceptionally meatlike. Because the fish is so big it is usually cut into steaks. Substitute fresh tuna.

Trout

A favorite freshwater sport fish (the season opens in April), but most today is hatchery raised. There are many types—e.g. brook, speckled, rainbow (native to California), and the larger lake trout. Flesh is sweet, firm and moist, moderate to high in fat. Trout is almost always served whole, but scales are so tiny that skinning is not usually necessary. Substitute bass, pike or salmon.

Tuna

A member of the mackerel family, fished from ancient times in warm to temperate parts of the Atlantic and Pacific. The largest specimens can be up to 12 feet long, while the smaller albacore tops out at 3 feet. Bluefin and big eye—darker and redder than albacore—are the varieties usually available in the market, but all types are interchangeable. The fish is usually cut into steaks; those cut from smaller fish are the easiest to work with. Much denser and oilier than most fish, tuna can well be compared to meat.

Turbot

Along with halibut, the largest of the flatfish. While halibut is strictly American, turbot is a European variety. Greenland turbot is frozen and imported. Though the typical market size is 18 to 20 inches, it can grow to 30 pounds. The fish is highly prized for its soft, lean white flesh. See *Flatfish.*

Whitebait

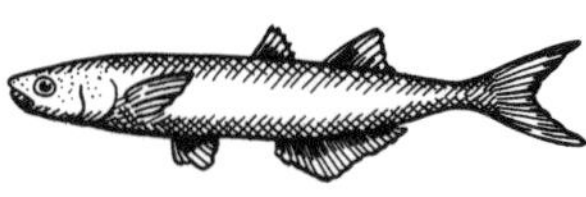

Can be any of several types of very small fish (sardines, silversides, herring, smelt) or the young of herring or sprats, typically deep-fried whole. The raw fish deteriorate quickly, so should be cooked soon after purchase.

Whiting

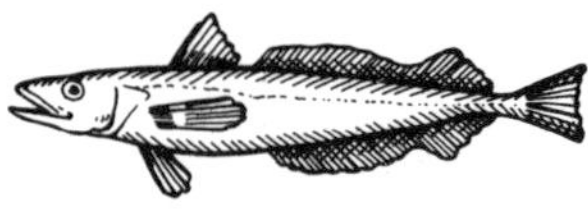

The market name for silver hake, a versatile member of the cod family. Caught in summer and early fall; ranges from Canada to Virginia. Average size is 12 to 18 inches and 1 pound, so it is convenient to serve one fish per portion. Flesh is delicate, lean and flaky; fish must be handled carefully to avoid breakage.

Yellow pike

The most important species of walleye, known also as zander. One of the best-eating freshwater fish, found in the Great Lakes and in European lakes. Typical market size is 1 to 3 pounds. Flesh is low-fat and firm. Substitute other pike, pickerel or perch.

Opposite: Quiche of Crabmeat and Endive (page 151).
Page following: Madison Avenue Stuffed Clams (page 112).

Whole Fish

Opposite: Medallions of Turbot with Apple (page 110).
Page preceding: Swordfish Pie Ajacienne (page 160).

Bluefish, Ile de France

Makes 4 servings

1 cup fresh breadcrumbs
1 tablespoon chopped fresh chives
1 tablespoon chopped fresh parsley
1 tablespoon chopped fresh tarragon
3 tablespoons olive oil
salt and freshly ground white pepper
1 whole $3^1/_2$-pound bluefish, cleaned and scaled
8 tablespoons (1 stick) butter, melted
juice of 2 lemons

In warm weather, bluefish is abundant along the East Coast. A favorite of sport fishermen, it should be gutted as soon as caught because it deteriorates quickly. As with all fatty fish, bluefish is best eaten as soon as possible after being caught; if you must freeze it, do it in a block of ice. Mackerel can also be used in this recipe.

1 Prepare charcoal grill. Combine breadcrumbs, herbs and $2^1/_2$ tablespoons olive oil in a bowl. Season with salt and pepper.

2 Stuff the fish through the gill cavity (see Note); season with salt and pepper. Brush the skin with the remaining $^1/_2$ tablespoon oil.

3 Place fish on the grill and cook for 6 minutes on each side. Meanwhile, preheat oven to 375°F.

4 When the fish has grilled for 12 minutes, remove and wrap in foil. Bake in the oven for 15 minutes. Serve hot.

Wine—Muscadet or California Sauvignon Blanc, served chilled.

Note: An interesting and efficient way of stuffing a fish is through the cavity of the gills, after they are removed. Place the stuffing in a pastry bag fitted with a plain tip and pipe it directly into the gill cavity, forcing it down into the body of the fish.

Carp with Ale

Ale and mustard here desert their old friend, the hot dog, for a member of the finny tribe. Accompany with baked potatoes. Perch can also be used in this recipe.

Makes 4 servings

2 tablespoons unsalted butter
2 tablespoons peanut oil
1 whole 3-pound carp
3 tablespoons chopped onion
1 stalk celery, chopped
1 tablespoon all-purpose flour
2 cups light ale
salt and freshly ground white pepper
1 tablespoon Dijon-style mustard

1 Heat butter and oil in a large skillet over medium heat. Add fish and cook for 10 minutes on each side, or until a knife inserted in the fleshiest part near the head leaves no trace of pinkness. Remove from skillet and keep warm.

2 Reduce heat to low and stir in onion and celery. Sprinkle with flour and sauté until golden. Add ale and cook gently for 15 minutes.

3 Return fish to skillet and season with salt and pepper. Cover tightly with aluminum foil and cook over medium heat for 15 minutes. Transfer fish to a platter.

4 Add mustard to the skillet and whisk constantly over gentle heat; do not allow mixture to boil. When mustard is well incorporated, pour sauce over fish and serve.

Serve with chilled ale, beer, or Muscadet.

Baked Carp with Herb Stuffing

Makes 4 servings

1 whole $2^1/_2$ pound carp

salt and freshly ground black pepper

3 tablespoons butter

2 shallots, minced

$^1/_2$ cup fresh breadcrumbs

1 teaspoon chopped fresh tarragon (or $^1/_2$ teaspoon dried)

1 teaspoon chopped fresh thyme (or $^1/_2$ teaspoon dried)

1 teaspoon chopped fresh parsley

1 teaspoon grated lemon zest

$^1/_4$ cup heavy cream

Carp is a freshwater fish found in rivers, lakes and ponds; the best-tasting grow in rivers. The fish originated in Asia and was exported first to Europe and eventually to the United States.

The scales on a carp are very tough, so it is best to have the fishmonger clean it. Serve with steamed new potatoes and lemon wedges. Perch can also be used in this recipe.

1 Scale and gut fish. Remove the head and reserve it. Season the fish with salt and pepper. Grease a baking dish large enough to hold the fish with 1 tablespoon butter.

2 Preheat oven to 375°F. Combine shallots and remaining 2 tablespoons butter in a small saucepan. Cover with a round of waxed paper and place a tight-fitting lid on the pan. Cook over low heat for 7 minutes. Remove from heat and add the breadcrumbs, chopped herbs, lemon zest and salt and pepper to taste. Stuff the cavity of the fish with this mixture.

3 Place the fish and head in the buttered baking dish. Bake for 20 minutes. Add cream and bake for an additional 10 minutes. Transfer fish to a heated platter. Replace head as if it were attached to body. Strain cream into a sauceboat and pass separately.

Wine—Meursault or California Chardonnay, served chilled.

Grilled Eel with Tartar Sauce

Eels begin life at sea, spend most of their lives in rivers and lakes and then return to the sea, where they spawn and die. They grow to maturity in fresh water, where they are usually caught. Serve grilled eel with a green salad. Dogfish can also be used in this recipe.

Makes 4 servings

1 cup homemade mayonnaise (see page 183)

1 hard-cooked egg, chopped

1 tablespoon chopped fresh parsley

1 tablespoon chopped shallot

1 tablespoon chopped capers

1 tablespoon chopped cornichons (small French sour pickles)

salt and freshly ground white pepper

1 2-pound or two 1-pound eels

1 tablespoon olive oil

1 teaspoon dried thyme

freshly ground black pepper

1 To prepare sauce: Place mayonnaise in a large bowl. Fold in egg, parsley, shallot, capers, cornichons, salt and pepper with a rubber spatula. Transfer to a sauceboat.

2 Preheat broiler or barbecue. Skin and wash eel; cut into 4 large pieces. Brush with olive oil and sprinkle with thyme, salt and black pepper. Broil or grill eel for 4 minutes on each side (3 sides in all). Then wrap the eel tightly in aluminum foil and cook for an additional 10 minutes.

3 Place eel on heated plates and pass the sauce separately.

Wine—Beaujolais or California Gamay Beaujolais, served cool.

Eels in a Dance of Herbs

Makes 4 servings

4 tablespoons unsalted butter
6 shallots, chopped
3 pounds eel, skinned and cut into 2-inch pieces
1 cup chopped sorrel
1 cup chopped spinach
1 cup chopped watercress
1 tablespoon chopped fresh parsley
1 tablespoon chopped fresh chervil
1 bunch tarragon
1 bunch mint
1 bunch sage
salt and freshly ground white pepper
4 cups dry white wine
2 egg yolks
juice of 1 lemon
½ cup heavy cream

The name of this recipe is inspired by the French ronde, *a circle dance. Here we have fish encircled by aromatic herbs. Plain rice is an excellent accompaniment. Dogfish can also be used in this recipe.*

1 Melt butter in a large non-aluminum pot over medium-high heat. Add shallots and eel and sauté for 5 minutes, stirring. Add vegetables, herbs, salt, pepper and wine, cover and cook over medium heat for 20 minutes.

2 Whisk egg yolks, lemon juice and cream and add to eel mixture. Stir until slightly thickened.

3 Place eel in center of heated plates and surround by herbs in sauce.

Wine—White Côte du Rhône, Cairanne or California French Colombard, served chilled.

Baked Flounder with Orange

Though both are flatfish and similar in appearance, sole and flounder belong to different families. Grey sole is not actually a sole, but a witch flounder. Lemon sole is a winter flounder. The only true sole available in the States are those imported from England and France. In any event, they can be used interchangeably. Although most Americans prefer to eat fillets, whole fish cooked with skin, head, tail and bones intact have flavor that cannot be duplicated. Serve this dish with steamed new potatoes.

Makes 4 servings

- *2 whole 2-pound flounder, cleaned and scaled*
- *2 tablespoons unsalted butter*
- *4 shallots, chopped*
- *salt and freshly ground black pepper*
- *2 cups dry white wine*
- *juice and grated zest of 2 oranges*
- *1 pound (4 sticks) cold unsalted butter*
- *3 oranges, peeled and divided into sections*
- *minced fresh parsley*

1 Preheat oven 450°F. Divide 2 tablespoons butter, cut into pieces, and the shallots between 2 gratin dishes. Place one flounder in each dish. Season with salt and pepper and add 1 cup wine to each dish. Bake for 15 minutes, or until a knife inserted into the fleshiest part near the head reveals no trace of pinkness or no flesh sticks to the bones.

2 Meanwhile, place the orange juice and zest in a nonaluminum saucepan and bring to a boil. Whisk in the pound of butter 1 tablespoon at a time. When the sauce has thickened, add the orange sections and cook just long enough to heat through.

3 To serve: Discard the skin from the flounder. Transfer the fish to a heated serving dish. Pour sauce over the fish and sprinkle with parsley.

Wine—Rosé Bellet or California Gamay Rosé, served chilled.

Kippers Mermaid

Makes 4 servings

---

2 cups milk
1 quart water
4 kippers or 2 pounds smoked haddock fillets
4 tablespoons unsalted butter, melted
4 tablespoons finely chopped mixed fresh parsley, chives and tarragon
3 tablespoons finely chopped roe of white-fleshed fish
1 cup finely chopped mushrooms
salt and freshly ground black pepper
3 tablespoons all-purpose flour
1/2 cup fresh breadcrumbs

Kippers are herring that have been brined and cold smoked. Smoked haddock is equally suitable for this dish. Serve with mashed potatoes.

1 Combine milk and water in a fish poacher. Add fish and bring liquid to a simmer. Poach gently for 30 minutes. Remove fish and set aside, reserving 1 cup of the cooking liquid.

2 In a bowl, combine melted butter, herbs, fish roe and mushrooms. Season with salt and pepper.

3 Preheat oven to 425°F. Place fish in a shallow baking pan. Spread herb mixture over fish. Sprinkle with flour, then breadcrumbs. Add reserved cooking liquid to pan. Bake for 8 minutes or until fish flakes easily. Serve hot.

Wine—Aligoté or California French Colombard, served chilled.

John Dory in Red Wine

In France, the very ugly but highly prized John Dory is known as St.-Pierre. This recipe came about in an unusual way. Ordinarily I would cook this fish in white wine. But one day I accidentally used red, and the results were so pleasing that I frequently prepare it now with red wine. I serve this dish with baked potatoes. Turbot can also be used in this recipe.

1 Clean and scale the fish and remove the fins.

2 Preheat oven to 250°F. Place the fish in a gratin dish. Add salt, pepper, shallot and wine and bake for 20 minutes. Discard the skin from the fish. Strain the cooking liquid into a nonaluminum saucepan and set fish aside in a warm place.

3 Boil the strained liquid until reduced to 2 to 4 tablespoons. Add the cream and boil for 10 minutes. Add the anchovy fillets and whisk in the butter 1 tablespoon at a time. The anchovies will disintegrate into the sauce.

4 To serve: Nap the fish with the sauce and sprinkle with the chopped chives.

Wine—Beaujolais Brouilly or California Zinfandel, served at room temperature.

Makes 4 servings

2 whole 2-pound John Dory

freshly ground white pepper

2 tablespoons chopped shallot

3 cups red wine, preferably a California Cabernet Sauvignon

3 cups heavy cream

2 anchovy fillets

4 tablespoons unsalted butter

1 bunch fresh chives, chopped

John Dory, My Way

Makes 4 servings

2 tablespoons unsalted butter

2 large onions, sliced

3 large Idaho potatoes, peeled and sliced paper-thin

2 whole 2½-pound John Dory, gutted, scaled and washed

1 cup fish fumet (see page 169)

pinch of saffron

2 cloves garlic, chopped

2 sprigs fresh thyme, chopped (or ⅛ teaspoon dried)

salt and freshly ground white pepper to taste

In other countries this is known as "St. Peter's fish." Although American John Dory is found in the Atlantic, it is not abundant enough to be fished commercially. In France, "St.-Pierre" is one of the classic ingredients of bouillabaisse. Turbot can also be used in this recipe.

1 Preheat oven to 425°F.

2 Melt butter in a medium skillet over medium heat. Add onions and sauté until golden but not brown.

3 Transfer onions to a large baking dish, spreading them out to make a bed for the fish. Arrange potatoes over the onions and place fish on top.

4 Combine fish fumet with saffron, stirring to dissolve saffron. Pour over the fish. Sprinkle with garlic, thyme, and salt and pepper to taste.

5 Bake for 35 minutes, or until fish is opaque and potatoes are tender. Serve directly from the baking dish.

Wine—Rosé de Provence or California Grenache Rosé, served chilled.

Mackerel on the Quay

This is the way mackerel is served in the small restaurants that dot the shores of France. Because of its oily quality and assertive flavor, mackerel is often cooked with an acidic white wine. Spoon some of the sauce over steamed rice. Fresh herring can also be used in this recipe.

Makes 4 servings

4 whole 1 1/2-pound mackerel
4 cups Muscadet
2 cups water
5 shallots, minced
3 cloves garlic, minced
2 bunches parsley
2 tablespoons unsalted butter
3 tablespoons all-purpose flour
1 cup heavy cream
salt and freshly ground white pepper
1/2 cup chopped fresh chives

1 Place mackerel in a pot large enough to contain the whole fish, preferably a fish poacher with a rack. Add wine, water, shallots, garlic and parsley. Bring to a boil; immediately reduce heat and simmer for 15 minutes. Carefully remove fish from broth and set aside in a warm place. Boil the broth until reduced to 2 cups.

2 Melt butter in a medium saucepan over medium heat. Whisk in flour and continue to cook, whisking, for about 2 minutes. Do not let flour brown.

3 Whisk in the broth and continue to whisk over medium heat until thickened. Add cream and cook for about 3 minutes over medium heat. Add salt, pepper and chives. Spoon sauce over fish and serve.

Wine—Muscadet-sur-lie or California Dry Chenin Blanc, served chilled.

Mackerel Marinated in Muscadet

Makes 4 servings

4 whole 1-pound mackerel
1 onion, cut into rings
2 carrots, peeled and sliced
3 cornichons (small French sour pickles), sliced
3 whole cloves
1 sprig fresh thyme (or 1/4 teaspoon dried)
1 bay leaf
5 white peppercorns
2 lemons, sliced and seeded
1 sweet red pepper
6 cups Muscadet
2 tablespoons white wine vinegar

Since mackerel is quite oily, it takes very well to marinating with wine, lemon or other acidic fruits. Be sure the mackerel you buy is absolutely fresh. Accompany this with crusty French bread. Fresh herring can also be used in this recipe.

1 Scale and gut the fish; remove fins and tails. Wash the fish and pat dry with paper towels.

2 Combine the fish with all remaining ingredients in a Dutch oven. Bring to simmer and cook gently for 30 minutes. Remove fish from liquid to cool. When both fish and liquid are cool, return fish to the liquid and refrigerate for several days before serving. Serve fish with some of the liquid and vegetables.

Wine—Muscadet or California Dry Riesling, served chilled.

Barbecued Mackerel with Roquefort Sauce

Mackerel, with its dark, oily meat, is particularly suited for marinating and grilling. If Roquefort is not available, there are any number of blue cheeses that can be substituted—Stilton, Danish, various French types and several premium domestic blues. Serve this dish with plain white rice. Fresh herring can also be used in this recipe.

Makes 4 servings

4 whole 1-pound mackerel
3 tablespoons Dijon-style mustard
1 tablespoon dry white wine
salt and freshly ground black pepper
1 cup fresh white breadcrumbs
1 cup fish fumet (see page 169)
1/4 cup heavy cream
1/2 cup crumbled Roquefort or other good-quality blue cheese
2 tablespoons unsalted butter

1 Scale mackerel; remove fins and tails. Wash well and pat dry with paper towels.

2 Whisk together the mustard, wine, salt and pepper. Pour this mixture over the fish and marinate for about 2 hours.

3 Coat the fish with breadcrumbs. Place on an oiled preheated barbecue grill and cook for 6 minutes on each side or until a knife inserted into the fleshiest part near the head reveals no trace of pinkness.

4 Boil the fish fumet in a small saucepan until reduced to 1/2 cup. Whisk in cream, cheese and butter. Taste and adjust seasoning with salt and pepper.

Wine—Bouzy Rouge or California Pinot Noir, served cool.

Red Mullet with Orange and Leeks

Makes 4 servings

5 tablespoons virgin olive oil

2 large leeks, white part only, cleaned and minced

3 cloves garlic, minced

2 onions, minced

1 stalk celery, minced

1 pound tomatoes, peeled, seeded and chopped

2 sprigs fresh thyme (or a pinch of dried)

1 bay leaf

zest (in strips) and juice of 1 orange

pinch of saffron

salt and freshly ground white pepper

1 cup water

8 red mullet, scaled but not gutted

juice of 2 lemons

1 bunch parsley, chopped

1 bunch chervil, chopped

On this side of the Atlantic red mullet is known as goatfish. In France, where it is called rouget, *it is traditional to cook and eat this fish without gutting. Serve with a rice salad made with sweet green or red pepper. Small red snapper can also be used in this recipe.*

1 Heat olive oil in a large saucepan over medium heat. Reduce heat to low and add leeks, garlic, onions, celery and tomatoes. Cover and cook for 15 minutes or until vegetables are softened but not browned.

2 Add thyme, bay leaf, orange zest and juice, saffron, salt, pepper and water and cook for an additional 15 minutes.

3 Preheat oven to 325°F. Arrange fish in a shallow baking pan. Spread sauce over the fish and bake, uncovered, for 20 minutes.

4 Cool, then refrigerate to chill. Sprinkle with parsley and chervil and serve cold.

Wine—Rosé Lirac or California Gamay Sauvignon, served chilled.

Mullet Saint-Tropez

Mullet is a favorite fish of the American South. Here we have a recipe from another South—the South of France. Steamed rice makes an excellent accompaniment. Red snapper can also be used this recipe.

Makes 4 servings

2 whole 2½-pound mullet, cleaned and scaled

salt and freshly ground black pepper

10 sprigs fresh tarragon (or 1 teaspoon dried)

7 tablespoons unsalted butter

2 fennel bulbs, sliced

4 ripe tomatoes, sliced

3 sprigs fresh thyme (or ⅛ teaspoon dried)

4 cloves garlic, minced

2 cups dry vermouth

¼ cup heavy cream

2 tablespoons chopped fresh chervil

1 Preheat oven to 400°F. Wash the fish and pat it dry with a paper towel. Salt and pepper the fish inside and out and place half the tarragon into the cavity of each.

2 Grease a shallow baking pan with 1 tablespoon of the butter, then scatter over it the fennel, tomatoes, thyme and garlic. Arrange the fish on top of the vegetables and pour the vermouth over it. Bake for 25 minutes, or until a knife inserted into the fleshy part just below the head reveals no trace of pinkness and no flesh sticks to the bones.

3 Remove the fish from the oven and strain the juices into a saucepan. Keep the fish and vegetables warm while preparing the sauce.

4 To prepare sauce: Boil the pan juices until they are reduced to 2 tablespoons. Add the cream and boil for 3 minutes. Whisk in the remaining 6 tablespoons butter, 1 tablespoon at a time.

5 To serve: Transfer the fish and vegetables to a platter. Serve the sauce separately in a sauceboat.

Wine—Rosé de Provence or California Chenin Blanc, served chilled.

Perch in Chardonnay

Makes 4 servings

4 whole 1-pound perch, scaled and gutted

salt and freshly ground white pepper

2 tablespoons olive oil

3 onions, chopped

1 pound tomatoes, peeled, seeded and diced

1 cup mushrooms, chopped

1 cup dry Chardonnay

2 tablespoons chopped fresh parsley

Although perch is generally a freshwater fish, it is also found in water of low salinity. In any case, its delicate texture and absorptive quality make it the perfect foil for this flavorful sauce. Serve this dish with rice. Pike can also be used in this recipe.

1 Preheat oven to 350°F. Rub fish with salt and pepper inside and out.

2 Heat olive oil in a skillet over high heat. Add onions and sauté 10 minutes.

3 Transfer onions to a shallow baking pan and top with fish. Surround with tomatoes and mushrooms. Pour wine over and bake for 20 minutes or until a knife inserted in the fleshiest part near the head reveals no trace of pinkness. Sprinkle with parsley and serve.

Wine—White Mercurey or California Chardonnay, served chilled.

Opposite: Shad Braised with Sorrel (page 48).
Page following: Monkfish Cake with Tomatoes (page 79).

Pike with Mushroom Scales

The creamy white sauce in this recipe looks like bechamel, but the shallots and mushrooms furnish their own assertive flavor. Roast potatoes (see next recipe) make an excellent accompaniment. (Photo opposite.)

Makes 4 servings

1 whole 3-pound pike, pickerel or perch
2 quarts court bouillon with white wine (see page 167)
2 tablespoons unsalted butter
4 shallots, chopped
1 cup mushrooms, sliced
2 tablespoons all-purpose flour
1 cup milk, heated to boiling
1 cup heavy cream
salt and freshly ground white pepper
pinch of nutmeg

1 Place fish in gently simmering court bouillon and simmer for 12 minutes.

2 Meanwhile, melt butter in a saucepan with tightly fitting lid. Add shallots and mushrooms and cook over low heat for 10 minutes. Stir in flour. Slowly whisk in milk; whisk gently for 7 minutes. Add cream and stir just until heated through. Season with salt, pepper and nutmeg. Transfer fish to a platter. Remove mushrooms with a slotted spoon and reserve. Pour sauce over fish and arrange mushrooms on fish to simulate scales.

Wine—Alsatian Sylvaner or California Sauvignon Blanc, served chilled.

Opposite: Pike with Mushroom Scales (page 35).
Page preceding: Sardines with Mint Napoleon (page 44).

Sweet-and-Sour Pike

Makes 4 servings

1 $2^1/_2$–3 pound pike, cleaned and cut into 1-inch slices

2 tablespoons kosher salt

2 tablespoons flour

1 tablespoon unsalted butter

2 cups red wine vinegar

1 bouquet garni, consisting of 1 bay leaf, 2 sprigs thyme, 1 stalk celery and $^1/_2$ bunch flat-leaf parsley

2 tablespoons red currant jelly

2 tablespoons raisins

2 tablespoons sliced almonds

$^1/_4$ cup sugar

2 tablespoons plus $^1/_2$ cup water

salt and freshly ground white pepper

2 tablespoons freshly grated or prepared horseradish

Good sauces have an almost universal application; sweet-and-sour sauce is no exception, as this dish amply demonstrates. Serve with steamed potatoes. Perch or pickerel can also be used in this recipe.

1 Place fish in a shallow dish and sprinkle with kosher salt. Let stand for 1 hour, then rinse and dry. Sprinkle with flour.

2 Melt butter in a large enamel or stainless steel skillet. Add fish, vinegar, bouquet garni, jelly, raisins and almonds and bring to boil. Cover, reduce heat to low and simmer for 1 hour.

3 Combine sugar and 2 tablespoons water in a small heavy saucepan and place over high heat. When the mixture starts to brown, stir constantly. When it turns dark brown, remove from heat and add remaining $^1/_2$ cup water. Return to heat, bring to boil and simmer for 5 minutes.

4 Add 6 tablespoons of this caramel coloring to cooking liquid. (Transfer remainder to a covered jar and store in refrigerator for another use.) Correct seasoning with salt and pepper. Transfer fish and sauce to a platter. Sprinkle with horseradish and serve.

Serve with chilled beer or dry white wine.

Grilled Yellow Pike in Shallot Sauce

A whole fish grilled over charcoal is bathed in a rich butter sauce. Serve this dish with baked potatoes.

1 Heat charcoal grill. Clean and scale fish. Brush fish with olive oil and season with salt and pepper. When coals are glowing, place fish on oiled rack and grill for 12 minutes on each side, or until a knife inserted in fleshiest part near the head reveals no trace of pinkness. Transfer to a serving platter and keep warm.

2 Melt butter in a saucepan over medium heat. Add shallots and cook until golden. Stir in parsley, egg yolks, lemon juice, and salt and pepper. Spoon over fish and serve hot.

Wine—Muscadet or California Dry Riesling, served chilled.

Makes 4 servings

1 whole 2½-pound yellow pike or perch

3 tablespoons virgin olive oil

salt and freshly ground white pepper

1 cup (2 sticks) unsalted butter

3 shallots, chopped

2 tablespoons chopped fresh parsley

4 hard-cooked egg yolks

juice of 2 lemons

Porgy with Bacon

Makes 4 servings

6 slices bacon, cut into 1/8 inch dice
2 tablespoons lard or peanut oil
6 shallots, minced
2 pounds boiling potatoes, minced
2 sprigs fresh thyme (or 1/8 teaspoon dried)
1 bay leaf
salt and freshly ground pepper
2 cups Alsatian Riesling
2 whole 1½-pound porgies
2 tablespoons unsalted butter
2 tablespoons chopped fresh parsley

In this unlikely combination, bacon adds its own rich flavor to mild-tasting, springy-textured porgy. Small grouper can also be used in this recipe.

1 Preheat oven to 375°F. Place bacon in a small saucepan, cover with cold water and bring to boil. Boil for 3 minutes, then drain and rinse under cold water.

2 Grease baking dish with the lard. Sprinkle on bacon and add shallots, potatoes, thyme, bay leaf, salt, pepper and wine. Bake for 30 minutes.

3 Salt and pepper the fish and arrange on top of the partially cooked vegetables. Dot with butter. Bake for 10 minutes. Turn and bake for an additional 10 minutes, or until fish is opaque. Transfer to a platter and sprinkle with parsley. Serve immediately.

Wine—Alsatian Riesling or California Chardonnay, served chilled.

Porgy Dauphinoise

Potatoes Dauphinoise always include cream. When the cream is replaced by fish stock, fish is added and the flavor is enhanced with aromatic herbs, we have all the ingredients of a delicious and healthful dish. Small grouper can also be used in this recipe.

1 Preheat oven to 375°F. Pour all but 2 tablespoons of the olive oil into a baking pan that will accommodate the fish and potatoes. Add half the parsley, potatoes and cheese to the pan. Place fish on top, sprinkle with thyme and add the bay leaf. Cover with remaining parsley, potato and cheese.

2 Pour on the fumet and sprinkle with reserved olive oil. Season with salt and pepper. Bake for 35 minutes. Serve hot.

Wine—Pouilly Fuissé or California Chardonnay, served chilled.

Makes 4 servings

1 cup virgin olive oil

1 whole 3-pound porgy, scaled and cleaned

6 large boiling potatoes, peeled and thinly sliced

6 tablespoons chopped fresh parsley

2/3 cup freshly grated Parmesan cheese

3 sprigs fresh thyme (or 1/8 teaspoon dried)

1 bay leaf

1 cup fish fumet (see page 169)

salt and freshly ground white pepper

Steamed Porgy with Seaweed

Makes 4 servings

2 pounds seaweed
salt and freshly ground black pepper
2 whole $1^1/_2$-pound porgies, cleaned and scaled
1 cup all-purpose flour
6 tablespoons water
juice of 2 lemons
3 tablespoons unsalted butter
freshly ground white pepper

Known in Europe as sea bream, porgy makes excellent eating and is usually eaten whole, not filleted. John Dory or turbot also works well in this recipe.

By sealing the pot with a paste of flour and water, all the flavor of the fish is retained. A wonderful aroma is given forth when the seal is broken. Unless you live near the sea and are familiar with the different varieties, it is best to get seaweed from the fishmonger; not all seaweed is edible. Serve this casserole with boiled potatoes.

1 Preheat oven to 425°F. Make a bed of half the seaweed in the bottom of a heavy Dutch oven or casserole. Salt and pepper the fish inside and out. Place it on top of the seaweed and cover the fish with the remaining seaweed.

2 Combine the flour and water to make a slightly sticky dough. Roll it into a rope 6 inches longer than the circumference of the casserole. Wet the edge of the lid and press dough around the top of the pot to form a seal. Bake for 20 minutes.

3 Meanwhile, heat lemon juice in a small nonaluminum saucepan. Whisk in butter 1 tablespoon at a time. Add salt and white pepper to taste.

4 Bring the casserole to the table and tap the crust to break the seal. Serve with lemon sauce.

Wine—White Aligoté or California Chardonnay, served chilled.

Porgy with Sea Urchin Sauce

Now that sea urchin roe is commercially available, recipes like this are within everyone's reach. Rinse the roe under cold running water before cooking. Baked potatoes are an excellent accompaniment. John Dory can also be used in this recipe.

1 Combine vegetables, bouquet garni, wine, olive oil, salt, pepper and enough water to cover fish in a fish poacher or a pot that can accommodate the fish. Bring to a boil, then reduce heat and simmer uncovered for 20 minutes.

2 Add the fish, cover pot and poach gently for 15 minutes. Allow fish to cool in the liquid.

3 Clean sea urchin roe. Combine with hollandaise and place in a sauceboat.

4 Remove fish from liquid. Arrange on plates and pass the sauce separately.

Wine—Muscadet or California Sauvignon Blanc, served chilled.

Makes 4 servings

1 large onion, sliced

1 carrot, peeled and sliced

2 stalks celery, sliced

1 bouquet garni, consisting of 2 parsley sprigs, 1/2 bay leaf, 1 sprig fresh thyme (or 1/8 teaspoon dried) and 1 stalk celery

4 cups dry white wine

1 tablespoon olive oil

salt and freshly ground pepper

2 whole 1 1/2-pound porgies, scaled and gutted

roe of 24 sea urchins

1 cup hollandaise sauce *(see page 181)*

Fresh Sardine or Herring Hors d'Oeuvres

Makes 4 servings

2 cups olive oil

2 tablespoons red wine vinegar

1 bouquet garni, consisting of 6 parsley sprigs, 1 bay leaf, 4 sprigs fresh thyme (or 1/4 teaspoon dried) and 4 sprigs fresh tarragon (or 1/4 teaspoon dried)

2 onions, minced

12 medium-size fresh sardines or 6 fresh herring

salt and freshly ground white pepper

Cold beer and potato salad with hard-cooked eggs are ideal accompaniments for this summer picnic specialty. The covering of olive oil safely preserves the fish.

1 Heat olive oil. Add vinegar, bouquet garni and onions and cook over low heat for 10 minutes.

2 Place fish in the hot oil and cook over low heat for 3 to 5 minutes. Season to taste with salt and pepper. Marinate for 2 days in a covered glass dish at room temperature. Drain well and serve.

Serve with chilled beer or dry white wine.

Fried Sardines France

This recipe is named for my grandmother, France, who was a great cook. It was she who inspired me to follow in her footsteps. Accompany each serving with steamed potatoes, deep-fried parsley (see next recipe) and a lemon half.

Makes 4 servings

2½ pounds fresh sardines or smelt

4 tablespoons unsalted butter

1 bunch parsley, chopped

6 shallots, finely chopped

salt and freshly ground white pepper

½ cup all-purpose flour

3 eggs

1 tablespoon Dijon-style mustard

4 cups peanut oil

1 Slit fish down the back and remove bones. Remove and discard heads, tails and fins.

2 Melt butter in a skillet over medium heat. Add parsley, shallots, salt and pepper and sauté until shallots turn golden. Stuff the fish with this mixture and press to close.

3 Preheat oil in deep-fryer to 355°F. Coat fish with flour. Beat eggs with mustard; dip fish into mixture. Plunge into the fryer for 3 minutes, or until crisp. Remove with slotted spoon and drain on paper towels. Serve hot.

Wine—Muscadet or California Sauvignon Blanc, served chilled.

Deep-Fried Parsley

Makes 4 servings

3 cups vegetable oil

2 bunches curly parsley, rinsed and dried

Preheat oil in a saucepan or wok to 375°F. Plunge parsley into oil ½ bunch at a time for 20 seconds. Remove with a slotted spoon and drain on paper towels.

Sardines with Mint Napoleon

Makes 4 servings

12 fresh sardines (about 1 pound)
1/2 cup chopped fresh mint
1/4 cup breadcrumbs
3 tablespoons virgin olive oil
salt and freshly ground pepper
juice of 1 lemon

In Corsica, where I was born, this dish is served as an appetizer with ratatouille (see page 54). The sardines can be baked or broiled. Small herring can also be used in this recipe. (Photo 3 following page 34.)

1 Slit sardines along the back and remove bones through the slit. Leave head and tail intact. Clean fish inside and outside; rinse and dry on paper towels.

2 Combine mint, breadcrumbs, olive oil, salt and pepper. Stuff the sardines from head to tail through the slit in the back. Roll up, starting at the tail.

3 Preheat oven to 400°F, or heat broiler. Place sardines in baking pan or on broiler rack. Bake for 6 minutes or broil for 3 minutes. Remove from heat and sprinkle with lemon juice. Serve hot.

Wine—Rosé de Provence or California Grenache Rosé, served chilled.

Roasted Red Snapper with Bay Leaves and Citrus

Since red snapper varies in size from small to 25 pounds or more, it can be prepared in many ways, from sautéed fillets to the large baked fish presented here. Serve this dish with parsley potatoes. Grouper or sea bass can also be used in this recipe.

Makes 4 servings

1 whole 5-pound red snapper, cleaned and scaled

8 bay leaves

salt and freshly ground white pepper

1 cup virgin olive oil

6 tablespoons water

3 oranges, peeled and divided into sections

5 limes, peeled and divided into sections

1 Preheat oven to 425°F. Place 2 bay leaves in the cavity of the fish. Break up the remaining bay leaves and ease them under the skin of the fish on both sides. Place the fish in a large baking pan. Season with salt and pepper and brush with 6 tablespoons olive oil. Add 6 tablespoons water to the pan. Bake for 30 minutes, adding more water if necessary.

2 Meanwhile, combine the remaining olive oil, salt, pepper and orange and lime sections in a saucepan and heat through but do not boil. Place in a sauceboat.

3 Transfer the snapper to a large platter and serve with the sauce.

Wine—Rosé de Provence or California Dry Rosé, served chilled.

Sea Bass with Honey Vinegar and Artichoke Bottoms

Makes 4 servings

$3^1/_2$ tablespoons virgin olive oil
2 carrots, chopped
1 onion, chopped
1 leek, chopped
2 stalks celery, chopped
shells of 4 lobsters
2 tablespoons Cognac
2 cups dry white wine
2 cups water
1 small head garlic, cut in half crosswise
2 ripe tomatoes, quartered
6 parsley sprigs
5 sprigs fresh thyme (or $^1/_4$ teaspoon dried)
$^1/_4$ cup honey vinegar
4 artichoke bottoms
2 tablespoons fresh lemon juice
2 whole $1^1/_2$-pound sea bass

Sea bass is found in both the Atlantic and Pacific Oceans. Its skin has an interesting black-and-white woven design, and its delectable white flesh is esteemed by chefs the world over. Honey vinegar can be found in specialty food shops. The artichoke bottoms should always be fresh, not canned. It's a bit tedious to remove all the leaves of the artichoke to obtain just the bottoms, but it is well worth the effort. Porgy can also be used in this recipe.

1 Heat 2 tablespoons of the olive oil in a large nonaluminum saucepan over very high heat. Add the carrots, onion, leek, celery and lobster shells and cook for a few minutes. Add Cognac, scraping up browned bits from bottom of pan. Add the wine, water, garlic, tomatoes and parsley and simmer for 1 hour. Strain the liquid and return to the saucepan. Boil for an additional 30 minutes over high heat until reduced to 1 cup. Mix in the thyme and vinegar and set aside.

2 Cook the artichoke bottoms in simmering salted water with lemon juice for 15 minutes, or just until tender. Drain and set aside.

3 Preheat the oven to 375°F. Wash and scale the fish and season with salt and pepper. Coat a shallow baking pan large enough to hold the fish with the remaining $1^1/_2$ tablespoons olive oil. Add the fish and bake for 20 minutes, or until a knife inserted into the fleshiest part near the head reveals no trace of pinkness and no flesh sticks to the bones.

4 Meanwhile, dice the artichoke bottoms. Sauté them over high heat in 2 tablespoons of the butter until slightly browned. Add the sliced lobster meat and cook for 5 minutes. Reheat sauce gently and add to the artichoke mixture with the remaining 1 tablespoon butter.

5 To serve: Arrange the sea bass on a serving platter and pour the artichoke-lobster mixture over it. Serve very hot.

Wine—Alsatian Pinot Noir or California Cabernet Sauvignon, served at room temperature.

salt and freshly ground black pepper

3 tablespoons unsalted butter

meat of 1 lobster (uncooked), sliced

Shad Braised with Sorrel

Makes 4 servings

1 whole 4-pound shad, cleaned and scaled

2 bunches fresh sorrel, chopped

3 slices white bread

3 tablespoons heavy cream

salt and freshly ground black pepper

5 tablespoons unsalted butter

5 shallots, sliced

1/2 cup Vouvray or sparking white wine

1/2 cup dry vermouth

1 cup heavy cream

1 bunch sorrel, thinly sliced

cooked rice

The eagerly awaited American shad is available only in the spring before June 1, when spawning begins. Shad is usually filleted because it has so many small bones, but if you prefer the whole fish, cooking it with sorrel dissolves the small bones. John Dory can substitute for shad when it is not in season. *(Photo opposite page 34.)*

1 Preheat oven to 425°F. Remove gills from fish. Rinse and pat dry with paper towels.

2 Combine chopped sorrel with white bread and 3 tablespoons cream. Season with salt and pepper to taste. Stuff both the stomach and gill cavities of the fish with this mixture. Cover openings with aluminum foil.

3 Butter a large baking dish; sprinkle with sliced shallots. Add fish and pour wine and vermouth over it. Dot with 1 tablespoon butter. Bake for 35 minutes, basting every 8 minutes. Set shad aside and keep warm. Pour contents of baking dish into a nonaluminum saucepan and boil until reduced to 3 tablespoons. Add 1 cup cream and simmer for 5 minutes. Whisk in remaining 4 tablespoons butter 1 tablespoon at a time. Strain sauce into a small saucepan and heat through. Season to taste.

4 Place shad on a nonaluminum tray or platter. Surround with sauce and arrange shredded sorrel over the sauce. Serve with rice.

Wine—Sparkling Vouvray or California champagne, served chilled.

Baked Red Snapper with Roasted Peanuts

The snapper family is one of the most important in the tropical seas. The most popular type, red snapper, is found in the South Atlantic from North Carolina to Brazil. It can grow to 35 pounds but the market size generally ranges from 1½ to 6 pounds. Serve this interesting creation with steamed white potatoes. Grouper or sea bass can also be used in this recipe.

Makes 4 servings

1 whole 2½-pound red snapper
1 lemon, sliced
2 tablespoons olive oil
1 onion, finely chopped
½ cup roasted unsalted peanuts
1 tablespoon chopped fresh parsley
white butter sauce (see page 179)

1 Preheat oven to 375°F. Remove bones from the whole fish through a slit in the back, leaving head and tail intact. Holding the fish horizontally, cut several vertical slashes about 2 inches apart, on one side only, and insert a lemon slice into each slit.

2 Cut a large piece of foil and spread with the oil. Place fish on foil and scatter the onion, peanuts and parsley on it. Fold foil in on all sides to enclose the fish. Place in a shallow baking pan and bake for 45 minutes. Transfer to a heated platter. Serve with white butter sauce.

Wine—Muscadet or California Sauvignon Blanc, served chilled.

Grey Sole Baked with Pearl Onions and Turnips

Makes 4 servings

1/2 cup all-purpose flour

salt and freshly ground black pepper

2 whole 2-pound grey sole, cleaned and skinned

3 tablespoons olive oil

16 pearl onions peeled

1/2 pound white turnips, cut into 1 1/2-inch dice

1 tablespoon unsalted butter

2 tablespoons finely chopped shallot

3 tablespoons red wine vinegar

1 teaspoon chicken stock base or 1/2 chicken bouillon cube

1/2 cup crème fraîche or heavy cream

8 tablespoons (1 stick) unsalted butter

2 tablespoons chopped fresh chervil

Although all sole are members of the founder family, each member possesses different attributes. The grey sole is very delicate in texture; unfortunately, its price at times drives it out of the market. Any other member of the flounder family can substitute for grey sole if it is unavailable or too expensive.

1 Combine flour with salt and pepper on a flat plate or waxed paper. Lightly coat the fish on both sides with the seasoned flour. Heat the olive oil in a cast iron skillet large enough to hold both fish (or using two skillets). Add the fish and brown lightly on both sides over medium-high heat.

2 Preheat the oven to 475°F. Add the pearl onions and place the skillet(s) in the oven for 12 minutes, or until a knife inserted into the fleshiest part near the head reveals no trace of pinkness.

3 Meanwhile, cook the diced turnips in boiling salted water for 6 minutes or until tender. Drain.

4 Transfer the cooked fish to a serving platter with the onions and turnips; keep warm. Melt 1 tablespoon butter in a sauté pan over medium-high heat. Add shallot and cook until soft. Add vinegar, chicken stock base and cream and boil until reduced by half in volume. Whisk in 8 tablespoons butter 1 tablespoon at a time. Spoon sauce over the fish, sprinkle with chervil and serve.

Wine—Meursault or Chenin Blanc, served chilled.

Opposite: Halibut Jacqueline in Champagne Sauce (page 75).
Page following: Stuffed Fresh Trout in Jail (page 57).

Sole with Beets and Capers

This recipe works well with a variety of flatfish—grey sole, lemon sole, Dover sole or plaice. Serve with steamed potatoes. (Photo opposite.)

Makes 4 servings

4 whole 1½-pound sole
1 cup milk
½ cup rye flour
4 tablespoons unsalted butter
salt and freshly ground pepper
1 medium beet, cooked, peeled and sliced
1 tablespoon capers
1 tablespoon chopped fresh parsley
2 lemons, halved
8 cornichons (small French sour pickles)

1 Wash and scale the fish. Dip in milk and coat with flour.

2 Melt 2 tablespoons butter in a skillet large enough to hold the fish (or use two skillets). Fry the fish over medium heat for 4 minutes on each side. Season with salt and pepper. Transfer to a platter and keep warm.

3 Heat remaining 2 tablespoons butter in a small saucepan until brown. Add beet and capers and sauté for 3 minutes over high heat, then pour over the fish. Sprinkle with parsley. Decorate the platter with lemon halves and cornichons. Serve hot.

Wine—A dry Rosé, or California Sauvignon Blanc, served chilled.

Opposite: Sole with Beets and Capers (page 51).
Page preceding: Stew of Brill with Vermouth and Tarragon (page 62).

Grey Sole Paysanne

Makes 4 servings

---

5 tablespoons unsalted butter

2 shallots, minced

1 onion, minced

1 carrot, peeled and sliced

1 teaspoon chopped fresh parsley

1 sprig fresh thyme (or a pinch of dried)

1 bay leaf

2 cups Cabernet Sauvignon

2 whole 1½-pound grey sole, skinned

½ cup sliced mushrooms

juice of 1 lemon

salt and freshly ground white pepper

2 tablespoons all-purpose flour

This dish is typical of the Gallic talent for making do with what every home has in its larder. Serve with steamed potatoes. Lemon sole or Dover sole can also be used in this recipe.

1 Preheat oven to 375°F. Melt 2 tablespoons butter in a skillet over high heat. Add shallots, onion, carrot, parsley, thyme and bay leaf and sauté, stirring, from time to time, for 10 minutes. Add wine and cook over medium heat for an additional 10 minutes.

2 Place the fish in a baking pan and pour on the wine sauce. Bake for 12 minutes.

3 Meanwhile, melt 1 tablespoon butter in a small saucepan. Add the mushrooms, lemon juice, salt and pepper and cook over medium heat for 5 minutes.

4 Transfer wine sauce to a saucepan and keep fish warm. Boil sauce until reduced by half; strain. Add mushrooms and bring to boil. Combine remaining 2 tablespoons butter with the flour to make a paste; add to the boiling sauce. Cook over medium heat for 7 minutes. Pour over fish and serve.

Wine—Beaujolais Villages or Cabernet Sauvignon, served at room temperature.

Baked Whole Grey Sole with Fresh Herbs

A recipe created for any large flatfish—Dover sole, plaice, brill, turbot or halibut. Serve with ratatouille (see next recipe).

Makes 4 servings

1 whole 3½-pound grey sole or other flatfish
2 tablespoons chopped fresh chives
2 tablespoons chopped fresh parsley
2 tablespoons chopped fresh tarragon
2 tablespoons chopped fresh sage
2 cups chopped mushrooms
3 shallots, chopped
1 cup dry white wine
½ cup water
1 sprig fresh thyme (or a pinch of dried)
1 bay leaf
salt and freshly ground white pepper
2 tablespoons unsalted butter
½ cup fresh breadcrumbs

1 Preheat oven to 375°F. Place the fish in a buttered shallow nonaluminum baking pan.

2 Combine chives, parsley, tarragon, sage, mushrooms and shallots. Scatter half the mixture around the fish. Add wine, water, thyme, bay leaf, salt and pepper.

3 Place remaining mushroom mixture on top of fish; dot with butter. Sprinkle with breadcrumbs. Bake for 35 minutes. Serve immediately.

Wine—Muscadet or California Fumé Blanc, served chilled.

Ratatouille

Makes 4 servings

3/4 cup (or more) virgin olive oil
1 large zucchini, diced
salt and freshly ground black pepper
1 medium eggplant (unpeeled), diced
1 large onion, chopped
3 large tomatoes, diced
2 cloves garlic, chopped
3 sprigs fresh thyme (or 1/2 teaspoon dried)
1 bay leaf

1 Preheat oven to 350°F. Heat 1/4 cup olive oil in a skillet over medium heat. Add zucchini and sauté for 10 minutes or until tender. Season with salt and pepper and transfer to a bowl.

2 Heat 1/4 cup olive oil in the skillet. Add eggplant and sauté for 10 minutes, adding more oil if necessary. Season with salt and pepper and add to zucchini.

3 Heat 1/4 cup olive oil; add onion and sauté until yellow and translucent. Add tomatoes, salt and pepper and cook until sauce has thickened, about 10 minutes. Combine with zucchini and eggplant.

4 Pour all the vegetables into a 2-quart baking pan; stir in the garlic, thyme and bay leaf. Cover and bake for 1 hour. Serve hot or cold.

Cold American Char Forestière

The delicate pink- or white-fleshed char, for which we usually substitute salmon trout, is the omble chevalier *found in the lakes of the French Alps. Ideal for summer dining, this dish can be prepared ahead. If char is not available, carp can also be substituted. If you can't find fresh cèpes, a few dried ones make an excellent substitute; alternatively, one or two dried cèpes added to common white mushrooms intensify their flavor. Serve with salad of cucumbers and tomatoes. Carp can also be used in this recipe.*

Makes 4 servings

1 whole 3-pound char or carp

2 quarts cooled court bouillon with white wine (see page 169)

2 tablespoons unsalted butter

1/3 cup minced cèpes or mushrooms

6 anchovy fillets in olive oil, minced

3 shallots, minced

4 hard-cooked egg yolks, minced

2 tablespoons minced cornichons (small French sour pickles)

2 tablespoons minced fresh parsley

juice of 1 lemon

2 tablespoons olive oil

salt and freshly ground white pepper

1 Place the fish in court bouillon and poach gently, without boiling, for 25 minutes. Cool in the liquid. Remove skin from fish. Transfer fish to a platter.

2 Melt butter in a small skillet and sauté cèpes over medium-high heat until all liquid has evaporated.

3 In a small bowl, mix cèpes, anchovies, shallots, egg yolks, cornichons and parsley. Stir in lemon juice and olive oil; season to taste with salt and pepper. Spoon over fish. Cover and refrigerate; serve chilled.

Wine—Juliénas or California Zinfandel, served at room temperature.

Smoked Salmon Trout Ulrich

Makes 4 servings

$2^1/_2$ quarts water
2 pounds sea salt
$2^1/_2$ pounds smoked salmon trout or smoked salmon, cut into 4 pieces
7 medium-size red potatoes
1 cup heavy cream
salt and freshly ground white pepper
3 tablespoons chopped fresh dill
Sweden sauce *(see page 188)*

My son Ulrich is particularly fond of this dish and when I'm too busy he occasionally prepares it himself. Despite the quantity of salt, the fish doesn't taste salty. Smoked haddock can also be used in this recipe.

1 Bring the water to a boil with the sea salt; stir to dissolve the salt. Remove from heat and cool. When the salt water is cool, add the smoked salmon trout and refrigerate for 48 hours. (This step will remove some of the smoky flavor.)

2 Cook the potatoes in boiling salted water until tender. Cut into 1-inch slices.

3 Pour cream into a saucepan and boil for 5 minutes. Add sliced potatoes, salt and pepper and simmer for 6 minutes. Sprinkle with dill, remove from heat and keep warm. Without removing the fish, bring salt water to a simmer and poach the fish for 8 minutes.

4 To serve: Place salmon in center of plate. Surround with a border of potatoes. Accompany with Sweden sauce.

Serve with chilled beer or aquavit.

Stuffed Fresh Trout in Jail

The trout in this recipe is "imprisoned" in foil, hence the fanciful name. Serve with steamed potatoes. Shad can also be used in this recipe. (Photo 2 following page 50.)

Makes 4 servings

6 tablespoons unsalted butter
1 pound mushrooms, finely chopped
juice of 1 lemon
salt and freshly ground black pepper
4 whole 1/2-pound trout
1 small carrot, peeled and minced
1 small onion, minced
1 stalk celery, minced
2 tablespoons water
4 sprigs fresh rosemary (or 1/2 teaspoon dried)
juice of 2 lemons

1 To make the stuffing, melt 2 tablespoons butter in a large skillet. Add mushrooms, juice of 1 lemon, salt and pepper and cook over medium heat for about 10 minutes, or until all the mushroom liquid has evaporated. Remove from skillet and set aside.

2 Wash trout and pat dry; season with salt and pepper. Place each trout on a square of aluminum foil.

3 In a skillet, melt 1 tablespoon butter; add the carrot, onion, celery, water and salt and pepper to taste. Cook over medium heat for 7 minutes. Drain and set aside.

4 Spoon the mushroom mixture into the cavities of the fish. Place the reserved vegetables over each fish and top with a rosemary sprig. Enclose the fish tightly in foil.

5 Preheat oven to 425°F. Place foil-wrapped fish on a baking sheet and bake for 10 minutes. Meanwhile, heat the juice of 2 lemons in a small nonaluminum saucepan over high heat. Whisk in remaining 3 tablespoons butter 1 tablespoon at a time. Adjust seasoning and serve with the fish.

Wine—Chardonnay from the Jura or California Chenin Blanc, served chilled.

Makes 4 servings

1/4 cup olive oil
2 bunches parsley, chopped
salt and freshly ground white pepper
4 whole 1-pound whiting, gutted and washed
1 medium Savoy cabbage, leaves separated
5 tablespoons unsalted butter
fast tomato sauce *(see page 189)*

Grilled Whiting and Savoy Cabbage

Whiting is a market name for the silver hake, a member of the cod family. With an average size of one pound, it is especially convenient as a single-portion fish.

Crinkly-leaved Savoy cabbage has a more delicate flavor than the common cabbage. Catfish can also be used in this recipe.

1 Prepare charcoal grill. Combine olive oil, parsley, salt and pepper and marinate fish in the mixture for 20 minutes.

2 Grill fish for 6 minutes on each side, basting with marinade from time to time. Preheat oven to 450°F.

3 Bring 2 quarts salted water to boil in a 4-quart pot. Drop in cabbage leaves, return to a boil and cook, covered for 7 minutes.

4 Drain cabbage leaves and spread in a rectangular baking pan. Dot with butter. Arrange fish on top of cabbage and season with salt and pepper. Bake for 10 minutes.

5 Divide fish and cabbage among plates and spoon on tomato sauce. Serve immediately.

Wine—Beaujolais Morgon or Zinfandel, served at room temperature.

Fish Fillets and Steaks

Striped Bass with Bacon Mediterranean Style

Makes 4 servings

12 slices bacon, julienned
2 pounds center-cut unskinned bass fillet, cut into 4 equal pieces
salt and freshly ground white pepper
20 basil leaves
1 tablespoon olive oil
10 small white onions, peeled and sliced
1/4 pound prosciutto, fat and lean, cut into julienne
3 cloves garlic
2 sweet green peppers, julienned
3 ripe tomatoes, peeled, seeded and chopped
2 zucchini, julienned

Striped bass is a great favorite of game fishermen. It is delicious served with pipérade, *a Provençal dish containing tomatoes and green peppers. A kind of pipérade is included here. Grouper can also be used in this recipe.*

1 Blanch bacon in boiling water for 10 minutes. Drain and rinse. Cut a horizontal pocket in each piece of fish. Season fish with salt and pepper. Stuff each fillet with several pieces of julienned bacon and 3 basil leaves. Top with additional bacon julienne and 2 basil leaves. Arrange in a baking dish and cover with foil.

2 Preheat oven to 450°F. In a large saucepan, heat oil, add onions and prosciutto and sauté over medium-high heat for 10 minutes or until golden. Add garlic and green peppers and cook until peppers are soft. Add tomatoes and zucchini, cover and simmer for 10 minutes. Bake bass until it is no longer transparent and it flakes easily, about 10 minutes. Serve on very hot plates, surrounding each fillet with the pipérade.

Wine—Rosé de Provence or California Grenache Rosé, served chilled.

Brill Corrick

Philip Corrick is chef at the Westbury Hotel in London; this is his recipe. For further information about brill, see the next recipe, Stew of Brill with Vermouth and Tarragon. Stilton, a blue-veined cheese from England, is the most popular of English cheeses to be found outside the British Isles. The flavor varies from very mild to strong, depending on the age. It is available in cheese shops and some supermarkets. Steamed potatoes are a good accompaniment to this dish. Halibut can also be used in this recipe.

Makes 4 servings

4 brill fillets (9 ounces each)
2 eggs, beaten
1/2 cup all-purpose flour
3 tablespoons unsalted butter
1 cup dry white wine
1/2 cup heavy cream
1/2 cup crumbled Stilton cheese
salt and freshly ground white pepper

1 Rinse fish and pat dry with paper towels. Dip each fillet into the egg, then coat with flour.

2 Melt butter in a large skillet over medium heat. Add fillets and sauté for 4 minutes on each side.

3 While the fish is cooking, bring the wine to a boil in a small nonaluminum saucepan; boil until reduced to 2 tablespoons. Reduce heat to medium and whisk in the cream; continue to whisk for about 3 minutes. Add the cheese and whisk until the sauce is creamy and smooth. Season to taste with salt and white pepper and spoon over the fish.

Wine—French Chablis or California French Colombard, served chilled.

Stew of Brill with Vermouth and Tarragon

Makes 4 servings

$2\frac{1}{2}$ pounds skinless brill fillets

5 tablespoons unsalted butter

$\frac{1}{2}$ cup dry white wine

$\frac{1}{2}$ cup dry vermouth

3 shallots, finely chopped

1 cup heavy cream

1 baking potato, baked and skinned, or $\frac{1}{4}$ cup dried potato flakes combined with $\frac{1}{4}$ cup water

salt and freshly ground black pepper

1 pound Belgian endive, cut into $\frac{1}{2}$-inch crosswise slices

2 tablespoons chopped fresh tarragon

Brill is a flatfish found in European and Atlantic waters. It lends itself to every style of cooking—baking, poaching, frying and, as here, stewing. Flounder or sole can be used in its place. (Photo 3 following page 50.)

1 Cut brill fillets into 2-inch strips.

2 Heat 3 tablespoons butter in a large skillet over high heat, until light brown. Add fish and sauté for about 4 minutes or just until opaque, turning once. Remove from pan with a slotted spoon. Set aside and keep warm.

3 Add the wine and vermouth to the pan and bring to boil over high heat, scraping up browned bits from bottom of pan. Add the shallots and continue cooking over high heat until 2 tablespoons liquid remain in pan. Add cream and boil for 4 minutes. Transfer the contents of the skillet to a blender or food processor together with potato pulp and blend until thick. Season with salt and pepper.

4 Melt remaining 2 tablespoons butter in a small saucepan. Add sliced endive and sauté for 2 minutes. Add salt and pepper to taste. Place the endive in the center of each heated plate. Arrange the fish over the endive and spoon on sauce. Sprinkle with tarragon and serve at once.

Wine—Chablis or California Chardonnay, served chilled.

Fresh Codfish Daudet

From the writer Alphonse Daudet's Provence comes this creamy version of brandade. *Made with fresh instead of salt cod, it is redolent of olive oil and garlic. Served with a salad, this is a great entrée. Haddock can also be used in this recipe.*

Makes 4 servings

2 pounds cod fillets
2 cups milk
2 cups water
2 bay leaves
5 cloves garlic, peeled
3 sprigs fresh thyme (or 1/8 teaspoon dried)
1 pound boiling potatoes
2 cups virgin olive oil
salt and freshly ground white pepper
3 tablespoons Niçoise olives

1 Combine fish, milk, water, bay leaves, garlic and thyme in a 4-quart pot and bring to simmer. Let simmer 12 minutes.

2 Boil potatoes in salted water to cover until tender. Drain, peel and mash. Remove fish from broth and combine with potatoes, mixing with a wooden spoon. Add enough of the cooking liquid to lighten the mixture. Beat in the olive oil, a very small amount at a time, mixing in each addition before adding the next as though making mayonnaise. After all the oil is incorporated, season to taste with salt and pepper.

3 Arrange brandade on a serving platter or in individual bowls and decorate with olives.

Wine—Rosé de Provence Bellet or California Grenache Rosé, served chilled.

Poached Codfish Fillets Chistera

Makes 4 servings

2½ pounds codfish fillets

2 quarts court bouillon with milk (see page 166)

3 tablespoons olive oil

1 large onion, minced

2 sweet red peppers, minced

2 small zucchini, minced

3 tomatoes, peeled, seeded and diced

1 bouquet garni, consisting of 1 bay leaf, 2 sprigs thyme, 1 stalk celery and ½ bunch flat-leaf parsley

2 cloves garlic, chopped

salt and freshly ground white pepper

3 tablespoons hollandaise sauce (see page 181)

This unusual recipe has an unusual name: a chistera *is the glove used in the Basque game of* pelote, *a form of jai-alai. Haddock can also be used in this recipe.*

1 Place fish in a large pot or fish poacher of gently simmering court bouillon and cook for 16 minutes. Meanwhile, heat olive oil in a large skillet over high heat. Add onion, red peppers and zucchini and sauté for 7 minutes.

2 Add tomatoes, bouquet garni and garlic and cook for 12 minutes more. Season to taste with salt and white pepper.

3 Remove bouquet garni. Place vegetables on a broiler-proof platter. Arrange fish over the vegetables and spoon on hollandaise sauce. Place under broiler for 3 minutes, or until lightly browned. Serve immediately.

Wine—Rosé de Provence or California Grenache Rosé, served chilled.

Codfish Père Claude

The sauce in this recipe is actually a variant of beurre blanc *(white butter sauce), except that it is made with red wine vinegar and red wine. Serve this dish with boiled potatoes. Haddock can also be used in this recipe.*

1 Place codfish in a pot with water, clam juice, parsley and carrot. Bring to a simmer and cook for 5 minutes. Remove fish from liquid and set aside, covered.

2 Combine shallots, vinegar and wine in a nonaluminum medium saucepan; boil until reduced by half (to about 3/4 cup). Add salt and pepper. Reduce heat and whisk in butter a tablespoon at a time, making sure that each tablespoon is incorporated into the sauce before adding the next one. Divide fish among heated plates and nap with sauce.

Wine—Same Beaujolais used in the recipe or a California Cabernet Sauvignon, served at room temperature.

Makes 4 servings

4 skinless codfish fillets (6 ounces each)

1 cup water

1 cup clam juice

2 tablespoons chopped fresh parsley

2 tablespoons chopped carrot

6 tablespoons minced shallots

1/2 cup red wine vinegar, preferably French

1 cup Beaujolais

salt and freshly ground white pepper

4 tablespoons unsalted butter

Codfish with Shallots and Red Wine

There has always been an abundance of cod in the oceans of the world, hence the great variety of recipes using it. Here we have the interesting combination of fish with a red wine rather than the very familiar white wine sauce. Buttered fettuccine makes a perfect accompaniment. Haddock can also be used in this recipe.

Makes 4 servings

5 tablespoons unsalted butter

6 shallots, chopped

2¾ cups light-bodied dry red wine

bouquet garni, consisting of 2 parsley sprigs, ½ bay leaf, 1 sprig fresh thyme (or ⅛ teaspoon dried) and 1 stalk celery

pinch of cinnamon

pinch of sugar

2 pounds codfish fillets

salt and freshly ground white pepper

2 tablespoons finely chopped fresh chives

1 Melt 1 tablespoon butter in a medium saucepan over high heat. Add the shallots and sauté for 5 minutes, or until translucent but not brown. Add the wine and bouquet garni and simmer for 20 minutes, or until reduced to 1¼ cups. Add the cinnamon and sugar and simmer for about 12 minutes, or until reduced to ⅓ cup. Set aside.

2 In a large skillet, melt 1 tablespoon of the remaining butter over high heat. Add the codfish and sauté for 5 minutes on each side, or until nicely browned.

3 Bring the reserved sauce to a boil and whisk in the remaining 3 tablespoons butter. Season to taste with salt and pepper. Place a portion of fish in the center of each serving plate and spoon the sauce over. Sprinkle with chives.

Wine—Beaujolais, Juliénas or California Zinfandel, served cool.

Opposite: Grouper with Three Vegetables (page 71).
Page following: Herring with Love Apples (page 77).

Flounder in Cider

The best cider to use for this recipe is the sparkling hard type, either French (from Normandy) or domestic. Regular apple juice is not appropriate; it is too sweet. Serve with steamed potatoes. Lemon sole can also be used in this recipe. (Photo opposite.)

Makes 4 servings

2 shallots, finely chopped

2 tablespoons unsalted butter

4 flounder fillets (6 to 7 ounces each), 1 inch thick

salt and freshly ground black pepper

1 1/4 cups hard cider, preferably French

2 large egg yolks

2/3 cup heavy cream

juice of 1/2 lemon

1 tablespoons chopped fresh parsley

1 Place shallots and butter into a large skillet and cover completely with a round of waxed paper cut to fit the pan. Cover with the pan lid and cook over low heat for 4 minutes. Add fish fillets, season with salt and pepper and turn to coat with the butter and shallots. Add the cider and poach gently for 12 minutes. Transfer the fish to a serving platter and keep warm.

2 Simmer the cooking liquid over medium heat until reduced by half. Transfer to a small saucepan. Whisk egg yolks and cream together and add to the reduced sauce, whisking over medium heat until thick. Add lemon juice and parsley and season to taste with salt and pepper. Spoon over the fish.

Beverage—French or domestic hard cider, served chilled.

Opposite: Flounder in Cider (page 67).
Page preceding: Pike Soufflé with Crayfish Sauce (page 81).

Flounder with Tomatoes and Sweet Garlic Sauce

Makes 4 servings

1 head garlic, peeled
3/4 cup virgin olive oil
2 onions, minced
4 ripe tomatoes, peeled, seeded and diced
6 sprigs fresh thyme (or 1/4 teaspoon dried)
2 tablespoons chopped fresh tarragon (or 1 tablespoon dried)
salt and freshly ground black pepper
1/2 cup all-purpose flour
1 tablespoon paprika
2 tablespoons unsalted butter
1 1/2 pounds skinless flounder fillets
1 tablespoon chopped fresh chervil

Flounder is one of the flatfish group. Excellent fillets also come from other members of the family—for example, lemon sole, Dover sole and sand dabs. Accompany this dish with small elbow macaroni. (Photo opposite page 3.)

1 Combine the garlic and 2 cups water in a small saucepan and boil for 15 minutes. Drain garlic, cool in ice water and drain again.

2 Heat 1/2 cup of the olive oil in a skillet over high heat. Add the onions and tomatoes and sauté until golden, about 5 minutes, stirring. Add garlic, thyme, tarragon, and salt and pepper to taste and simmer for 8 minutes. Discard the thyme. Puree the mixture in a blender or food processor and return to the saucepan.

3 Combine the flour and paprika on a flat plate. Salt and pepper the fish fillets and coat them with the seasoned flour, shaking off excess. In a skillet heat 2 tablespoons butter and the remaining 1/4 cup olive oil over high heat. Add the fish and sauté until browned, about 3 minutes on each side.

4 Reheat the sauce. Place fish fillets on 4 plates, spoon hot sauce over and sprinkle with chervil.

Wine—Juliénas or California Gamay Beaujolais, served cool.

Grilled Grouper with Creamed Leeks

Although a tropical species, grouper is available at fish stores throughout the United States. The creamy leeks and pungent mustard make for an interesting marriage of flavors. Serve with steamed potatoes. Brill can also be used in this recipe.

Makes 4 servings

4 grouper fillets (6 ounces each)

1 teaspoon dry white wine

3 tablespoons Dijon-style mustard

1/2 cup water

2 tablespoons unsalted butter

salt and freshly ground black pepper

3 large leeks, white and pale green parts only, thinly sliced

1/2 cup heavy cream

2 lemons, halved

1 Preheat broiler or prepare barbecue grill. Wash fish and pat dry with paper towels. Combine wine and mustard and brush fish with this mixture. Cook fish for 5 minutes on each side. Transfer to a platter and cover with aluminum foil to keep warm.

2 Bring water to boil in a large skillet with butter, salt and pepper. Add sliced leeks and cook uncovered for 6 minutes. Add cream and boil for 3 more minutes.

3 Place leek mixture in the center of 4 heated plates and top with fish fillets. Decorate each plate with half a lemon.

Wine—Aligoté or Sauvignon Blanc, served chilled.

Grouper Fillet Madras

Makes 4 servings

2 tablespoons unsalted butter
3 tomatoes, peeled, seeded and diced
2 onions, chopped
1 bunch parsley, chopped
2 cloves garlic, minced
2 teaspoons curry powder
2½ pounds skinless grouper fillets
salt and freshly ground white pepper
1 cup dry white wine

A hint of India gives this dish its distinctive flavor. Brill can also be used in this recipe.

1 Preheat oven to 375°F. Using 2 tablespoons butter, grease a shallow baking dish large enough to hold the fish in a single layer. Arrange the tomatoes, onions, parsley and garlic over the bottom. Sprinkle with curry powder and place the fish on top. Season with salt and pepper and add the wine.

2 Bake, uncovered, for 30 minutes. Serve hot.

Wine—Aligoté or California Sauvignon Blanc, served chilled.

Grouper with Three Vegetables

A warm-water fish, grouper is found in the Atlantic and in the warmer parts of the Mediterranean. Large grouper provides steaks; the smaller ones can be eaten whole or filleted. Brill can also be used in this recipe. *(Photo opposite page 66.)*

Makes 4 servings

3 ripe tomatoes
1 cucumber, unpeeled
4 grouper fillets (7 ounces each)
1/2 pound medium mushrooms, sliced
salt and freshly ground white pepper
4 sprigs fresh dill
3 tablespoons water
cooked rice
fast tomato sauce (see page 189)

1 Prepare barbecue grill or preheat oven to 400°F. Plunge tomatoes into boiling water for 20 seconds. Rinse under cold water, then peel and slice. Slice the cucumber. Cut 4 squares of aluminum foil large enough to accommodate each portion of fish and vegetables.

2 Arrange the fish and vegetables in horizontal rows, one alongside the other, as follows: fish, mushrooms, tomatoes, cucumbers. Salt and pepper to taste. Place a sprig of dill on top and sprinkle 3/4 teaspoon water over contents of each package. Bring edges of foil up and close packages very tightly with double folds. Place on baking sheet or in covered barbecue and cook 14 minutes. Present in package. Serve with rice and tomato sauce.

Wine—Red Mercurey or California Zinfandel.

Sautéed Haddock Mme. Colette

Makes 4 servings

---

1 pound boiling potatoes, unpeeled

6 tablespoons unsalted butter

3 pounds haddock fillets

salt and freshly ground white pepper

3 onions, minced

2 tablespoons chopped fresh parsley

3 tablespoons red wine vinegar

My mother, for whom this dish is named, displayed her creative turn of mind in the kitchen. Actually a layered fish hash, this is a perfect example of her inventiveness. Cod can also be used in this recipe.

1 Cook potatoes in boiling salted water for about 25 minutes or until tender but still firm.

2 Meanwhile, melt 3 tablespoons butter in a large nonaluminum skillet over medium heat. Sauté the fish for 6 minutes on each side, or until it is white and opaque. Season with salt and pepper. Remove from pan, flake and keep warm.

3 Melt the remaining 3 tablespoons butter in the same skillet over medium heat. Add the onions and sauté until tender, about 10 minutes. Cut the potatoes into 1/4-inch slices and add to the skillet without stirring. Top with the fish flakes and cook for 6 minutes without stirring.

4 Transfer mixture onto individual plates with a spatula and sprinkle with parsley. Pour vinegar into the hot skillet and bring to a boil, scraping up browned bits. Boil briefly and pour over the fish. Serve immediately.

Wine—Moulin à Vent or California Zinfandel, served at room temperature.

Haddock and Potato Gratin

The haddock is a smaller member of the cod family; their uses are interchangeable. Smoked haddock, also known as finnan haddie, originated in Scotland. In this country, most finnan haddie is processed in New England.

Makes 4 servings

3/4 pound fresh haddock fillets

1 pound smoked haddock fillets

1 cup milk

1 bay leaf

1 sprig fresh thyme (or 1/4 teaspoon dried)

2 pounds boiling potatoes, peeled and cut into chunks

5 tablespoons butter

2 tablespoons all-purpose flour

salt and freshly ground black pepper

4 hard-cooked eggs, chopped

2 tablespoons chopped fresh tarragon

2 tablespoons chopped fresh parsley

1 Preheat oven to 325°F. Place both fish in an enamel baking pan together with the milk, bay leaf and thyme. Cover with foil and bake for 15 minutes. While the fish is baking, cook the potatoes in a pot of salted water until soft enough to mash.

2 Remove fish from pan, leaving the liquid. Increase oven heat to 450°F and return pan to oven until liquid is reduced by half, about 10 minutes. Carefully flake the fish, being careful to remove all bones.

3 Melt 3 tablespoons of the butter in a saucepan over low heat. Whisk in flour. Add reduced fish liquid and simmer for 8 minutes, whisking constantly.

4 Mash the potatoes and season with salt and pepper. Place the fish in a gratin dish. Spoon on the sauce. Sprinkle with the hard-cooked eggs, tarragon and parsley. Cover with mashed potatoes and dot with remaining 2 tablespoons butter. Bake at 450°F for 15 minutes or until slightly browned.

Wine—A Portuguese Rosé or California Fumé Blanc, served chilled.

Raw Halibut with Pernod

Makes 4 servings

$1\frac{1}{2}$ pounds very fresh halibut fillets
juice of 3 limes
2 tablespoons Pernod
salt and freshly ground black pepper
8 whole star anise
2 lemons, sliced
fresh dill sprigs

When fish is eaten raw, it must be impeccably fresh. Star anise, used only as a garnish in this recipe, reflects the Pernod which is the predominant flavor of the dish. Star anise, as its name implies, is a star-shaped spice. Always found in Chinese grocery stores, it is now available in the specialty sections of many supermarkets. In Provence, huge sacks of star anise are to be found among all the other spices at many of the outdoor weekly markets.

Serve this halibut with potato salad for a refreshing light meal. Sea bass can also be used with this recipe.

1 Cut halibut fillet into very thin slices. Combine the lime juice and Pernod; add salt and pepper. Brush mixture over both sides of fish slices and arrange attractively on a chilled platter.

2 Boil the star anise in 2 cups of water for 5 minutes. Drain and chill in cold water. Use as a decoration on fish platter, together with lemon slices and dill sprigs.

Wine—Rosé de Provence or California Grenache Rosé, served chilled.

Halibut Jacqueline in Champagne Sauce

This can be cooked under an oven broiler or on an indoor or outdoor charcoal grill. Jacqueline is my wife's best friend, and this is her favorite dish. Sea bass can also be used in this recipe. (Photo opposite page 50.)

Makes 4 servings

$1^1/_2$ pounds halibut fillets
$^2/_3$ cup Champagne
1 pound bay scallops
$^2/_3$ cup crème fraîche
8 tablespoons (1 stick) unsalted butter
salt and cayenne pepper
$^1/_4$ cup peanut oil
freshly ground white pepper
1 ounce salmon roe

1 Rinse the halibut fillets under cool water and pat them dry with paper towels. In a large non-aluminum saucepan, bring the Champagne to a boil. Add the scallops and cook for 3 minutes. Remove the scallops from the liquid with a slotted spoon and set aside.

2 Boil the cooking liquid for about 15 minutes, or until reduced to about 3 tablespoons. Whisk in the crème fraîche, then remove from heat and whisk in the butter. Set aside.

3 Preheat the broiler or charcoal grill. Sprinkle salt and cayenne pepper on both sides of the fish fillets and brush with the peanut oil. Broil for 4 minutes on each side. Remove and keep warm. Reheat the sauce gently and season to taste with salt and pepper.

4 To serve: Ladle sauce onto 4 plates. Place the grilled fish in the center, dividing it evenly. Arrange the scallops in a large circle around the fish. Top the fish with a dab of salmon roe.

Wine—Sparkling Vouvray, French Champagne or California Champagne, served chilled.

Halibut with Walnuts Pappy Claude

Makes 4 servings

3 pounds halibut, cut into 1-inch-thick steaks

2 quarts cooled court bouillon with milk (see page 166)

2 cloves garlic, minced

6 anchovy fillets, finely chopped

1/2 cup chopped walnuts

1 1/2 cups homemade mayonnaise (see page 183)

Halibut is a favorite of my father-in-law's, and this preparation is one that he most enjoys. A Bibb lettuce salad makes an excellent side dish. Sea bass can also be used in this recipe.

1 Place fish in court bouillon and bring to a simmer; let simmer for 8 minutes. Remove from heat and keep fish warm in the liquid.

2 In a bowl, combine garlic, anchovies, walnuts and mayonnaise. Remove skin from fish, arrange on a platter and cover with sauce. Serve immediately.

Wine—Chablis or California Sauvignon Blanc, served chilled.

Herring with Love Apples

The tomato, a fruit of South American origin, was given the romantic name "love apple" when it was first introduced to Europe.

Herring, probably the most plentiful of fish, are not too often prepared fresh in our part of the world. But salted, pickled, kippered and canned, they are enormously popular—and also quite high in oil content, which makes them very desirable to the health-conscious. Fresh sardines can also be used in this recipe. *(Photo 2 following page 66.)*

Makes 4 servings

6 fresh herring (1 pound each), heads removed, filleted
1 small onion, chopped
1 small carrot, peeled and chopped
1 teaspoon tomato paste
5 ripe tomatoes
1 teaspoon dried thyme
1 tablespoon prepared horseradish
juice of 1 lemon
1/2 cup dry white wine
1 teaspoon sugar
2 tablespoons virgin olive oil
salt and freshly ground black pepper
cooked spaghetti

1 Place herring fillets in a dish or casserole. Combine all remaining ingredients except spaghetti in a large saucepan and bring to a simmer. Cook for 20 minutes. Immediately transfer to a food processor and puree. While still hot, pour the sauce over the herring. Cover and marinate in the refrigerator for 48 hours.

2 To serve: Reheat herring and sauce. Serve over spaghetti.

Serve with Chianti or cold beer.

Roast Monkfish with Sorrel

Makes 4 servings

1½ pounds fresh sorrel
2½ pounds monkfish fillet
2 cups Muscadet
1 cup heavy cream
salt and freshly ground white pepper
2 egg yolks
2 tablespoons unsalted butter

The tail is the only edible part of a monkfish. Removing the backbone leaves two perfect boneless fillets. Steamed potatoes are a good mate for this dish. Skate can also be used in this recipe.

1 Preheat oven to 325°F. Spread sorrel in a large nonaluminum baking pan. Arrange fish on the sorrel and add wine, cream, salt and pepper. Bake for 25 minutes, or until fish is opaque. Transfer sorrel and fish to a heated platter and keep warm.

2 Pour sauce into saucepan and whisk in egg yolks. Continue to whisk over medium heat until sauce thickens, about 5 minutes; do not boil. Remove from heat and stir in butter. Spoon sauce over fish and serve immediately.

Wine—Muscadet or California Chardonnay, served chilled.

Monkfish Cake with Tomatoes

Monkfish, also known as goosefish, is an ugly but delicate-tasting species. This cold dish combines monkfish with fresh, ripe tomatoes. Served with a green salad, it is ideal for summertime dining. Skate can also be used in this recipe. *(Photo 2 following page 34.)*

Makes 4 servings

2 pounds monkfish

4 cups fish fumet *(see page 169)*

1/4 cup virgin olive oil

2 pounds ripe tomatoes, peeled, seeded and cut into large chunks

2 sprigs fresh thyme (or 1/8 teaspoon dried)

2 cloves garlic, chopped

salt and freshly ground white pepper

8 eggs, beaten

1 Remove membrane that adheres to flesh of the monkfish. Combine the fish and fumet in a nonaluminum saucepan. Bring the fumet to a simmer and poach the fish gently for 20 minutes.

2 While the fish is cooking, heat olive oil in a large skillet over high heat. Add tomatoes, thyme and garlic and sauté for 8 minutes, stirring occasionally. Season with salt and pepper; remove from heat.

3 Remove fish from the broth and cut into 1/8-inch dice. Combine with tomatoes and eggs. Spoon the mixture into a buttered 6-cup mold. Refrigerate for 30 minutes.

4 Preheat oven to 400°F. Place mold in a baking pan; add hot water to reach halfway up sides of mold. Bake for 50 minutes or inserted knife comes out clean.

5 Remove mold from water bath and cover with aluminum foil. Top with a weight (such as a few cans of food) and bring to room temperature. Refrigerate for at least one day before unmolding and slicing.

Wine—French Chablis or California Chenin Blanc, served chilled.

Pike Poached in Champagne

Makes 4 servings

2 pounds pike fillets
4½ cups court bouillon (see page 167)
2½ cups Champagne
3 egg yolks
½ cup heavy cream
8 tablespoons (1 stick) butter
salt and freshly ground white pepper
juice of 1 lemon

Royalty marries royalty in this union of a great freshwater fish and a great wine. Serve with steamed potatoes. Perch can also be used in this recipe.

1 Combine fish, 4 cups court bouillon and 2 cups Champagne in a fish poacher with rack (or wrap fish in cheesecloth, to facilitate removal, and use a large saucepan). Bring liquid to a simmer and poach fish for 20 minutes.

2 In a small nonaluminum saucepan combine remaining ½ cup court bouillon with remaining ½ cup Champagne and boil until reduced by ⅔. Combine egg yolks with cream and whisk into the reduced liquid. Simmer gently for 5 minutes.

3 Whisk in butter a tablespoon at a time, making sure that each is incorporated before adding the next. Season sauce to taste with salt and pepper and add lemon juice. Arrange fish on heated plates and spoon on sauce.

Wine—French or California Champagne, served chilled.

Pike Soufflé with Crayfish Sauce

The preparation of this dish is painstaking but not really difficult. The results are well worth the effort; it makes a truly elegant first course. Perch can also be used in this recipe. (Photo 3 following page 66.)

Makes 4 servings

1 pound skinless pike fillets

salt and freshly ground white pepper

3 egg yolks

3 whole eggs

12 tablespoons (1½ sticks) unsalted butter, melted

1 cup heavy cream

1 cup sauce Américaine (page 176), substituting crayfish for lobster

1 Combine fish, salt and pepper in a food processor and blend for 3 minutes, stopping from time to time to scrape down the sides of the bowl. Add egg yolks and process for a few seconds, then add whole eggs and pulse a few times to combine. Add melted butter and process for 1 minute.

2 Transfer to a mixing bowl and gently stir in cream. Cover and refrigerate the mixture for 1 hour.

3 Preheat oven to 350°F. Divide fish mixture among 4 buttered individual soufflé molds. Place in a pan of hot water and bake for 15 minutes.

4 Remove from oven, scoop out a spoonful of soufflé from each mold and fill with sauce. Pass remainder of sauce in a sauceboat.

Wine—Macon or California Chardonnay, served chilled.

Poached Yellow Pike with Chives

Makes 4 servings

2 carrots, peeled and minced

1 large onion, minced

3 shallots, minced

1 bouquet garni, consisting of 1 bay leaf, 2 sprigs thyme, 1 stalk celery and 1/2 bunch flat-leaf parsley

1 cup Muscadet

1 cup water

salt and freshly ground white pepper

3 pounds yellow pike fillets

1/2 cup heavy cream

2 tablespoons unsalted butter

2 bunches chives, finely chopped

The most important species of walleye is know as zander or yellow pike. The best are found in our Great Lakes and in lakes throughout Europe. Perch can also be used in this recipe.

1 Combine carrots, onion, shallots, bouquet garni, wine, water, salt and pepper in a nonaluminum saucepan and boil for 20 minutes. Let cool.

2 Place fish fillets in cooled bouillon and bring to a gentle simmer. Poach for 8 minutes. Remove fish from liquid and keep warm. Bring liquid to a boil; continue to boil until reduced by half.

3 Add cream and boil for an additional 6 minutes. Strain through a fine sieve into another saucepan, pressing down on the solids to extract as much flavor as possible.

4 Whisk in butter and chives over low heat. Spoon sauce over fish and serve at once.

Wine—Muscadet or California Chenin Blanc, served chilled.

Opposite: Salmon Marinated with Olive Oil and Herbs (page 86).
Page following: Wild Salmon Paillard Karine (page 88).

Poached Pollack Onzainoise

Onzain is the town in the Loire where, starting at the age of 12, I was apprenticed. Serve this dish with golden rice, a variety obtainable at specialty food shops. White rice can be used as an alternate. Cod can also be used in this recipe.

1 Place fish in water to cover in a large saucepan. Season with thyme, salt and pepper and poach gently for 8 minutes. Remove fish from liquid. Flake when cool enough to handle.

2 Heat olive oil in a skillet over high heat. Add onions and sauté until golden. Add tomatoes, garlic, parsley, salt and pepper and cook gently for 10 minutes.

3 Combine mixture with fish, capers and olives and serve.

Wine—Rosé de Provence, Côtes de Bellet or California Grenache Rosé, served chilled.

Makes 4 servings

3 pounds pollack fillets
1 sprig fresh thyme (or a pinch of dried)
salt and freshly ground white pepper
3 tablespoons olive oil
2 onions, minced
1 cup peeled, seeded and diced tomatoes
2 cloves garlic, chopped
1 teaspoon chopped fresh parsley
1 tablespoon capers
3 tablespoons pitted oil-cured black olives

Opposite: Red Snapper Baked Alaska (page 95).
Page preceding: Ceviche of Fish (page 94).

Pompano Fillets with Scallion

Makes 4 servings

FISH FUMET

1 tablespoon unsalted butter

1/4 cup chopped carrot

1 tablespoon chopped shallot

1/4 cup chopped onion

bones from 2 whole pompanos

2 1/2 cups (about) cold water

1 teaspoon chicken stock base or 1/2 chicken bouillon cube

4 pompano fillets (from two 2-pound pompanos)

salt and freshly ground white pepper

5 tablespoons unsalted butter

10 scallions, chopped

4 sprigs fresh thyme

8 basil leaves

Many aficionados think pompano is the best fish found in the southern Atlantic. Serve this with sautéed potatoes (see next recipe). Red snapper can also be used in this recipe.

1 To prepare the fish fumet: Melt 1 tablespoon butter in a 2-quart pot over high heat. Add the carrot, shallot and onion and cook for a few minutes, then add the fish bones and cold water, making sure there is enough water in the pot to cover the bones. Boil for about 20 minutes or until reduced to 1/2 cup. Set aside.

2 Preheat broiler. Wash the fish fillets under cool water and pat dry with paper towels. Season with salt and pepper. Melt 1 tablespoon butter in a small skillet. When hot, add the scallions and sauté just until softened. Divide the scallions equally among 4 individual gratin dishes. Place a fish fillet over the scallions in each dish and coat with some of the fish fumet. Whisk rest of butter with the remaining fumet. Garnish with thyme and basil. Broil for 1 minute, then serve immediately.

Wine—Tavel Rosé or Gamay Beaujolais, served chilled.

Sautéed Potatoes

1 Rinse potatoes in cold water and dry with paper towels. Season with salt and pepper.

2 Heat oil and butter in a large skillet over high heat. Sauté potatoes on both sides until golden brown, approximately 10 minutes. Serve hot.

Variations:
For Potatoes Lyonnaise, sauté 1 large chopped onion in the oil and butter until tender. Add potatoes and proceed with recipe.

For Potatoes Provençale, sauté 1 large chopped onion in the oil and butter until tender. Add 2 cloves chopped garlic cloves and a pinch of dried thyme and sauté briefly. Add potatoes and proceed with recipe.

Makes 4 servings

---

6 Idaho baking potatoes, sliced 1/16 inch thick

salt and freshly ground white pepper

2 tablespoons virgin olive oil

2 tablespoons unsalted butter

Salmon Marinated with Olive Oil and Herbs

Makes 4 servings

$1^1/_2$ pounds very fresh salmon fillets

$^1/_2$ cup virgin olive oil

juice of 2 lemons

1 tablespoon Dijon-style mustard

salt and freshly ground pepper

1 teaspoon chopped fresh dill

1 teaspoon chopped fresh tarragon

1 teaspoon chopped fresh chervil

1 teaspoon chopped fresh chives

sliced mushrooms

Since the salmon in this recipe is uncooked, be sure to purchase it from a reliable fishmonger where freshness is assured. Serve this dish with a salad of sliced mushrooms dressed with the leftover marinade. Salmon trout can also be used in this recipe. (Photo opposite page 82.)

1 Cut the salmon fillets at an angle into large, very thin slices. Combine olive oil, lemon juice, mustard, salt and pepper. Place salmon in this mixture, sprinkle herbs on top and marinate for 10 minutes on each side.

2 To serve, divide salmon slices among 4 chilled plates. Decorate with sliced mushrooms.

Wine—Meursault or California Chardonnay, served chilled.

Gravlax

Swedish in origin, this treatment results in salmon with a delicate taste and fine texture. Slice thinly and serve with pumpernickel as a first course or as part of a buffet; accompany with Sweden sauce (see page 188). Salmon trout can also be used in this recipe.

Makes 4 servings

2 1/2 pounds fresh salmon fillets, skin on

10 ounces coarse kosher salt

1 1/2 cups sugar

3 tablespoons coarsely cracked white pepper

1/2 cup finely chopped fresh dill

1 Wash salmon fillets and pat dry with a paper towel. Place in a shallow dish, skin side down. Combine salt, sugar and pepper and sprinkle on fish together with chopped dill.

2 Cover with plastic wrap and refrigerate for 48 hours, turning from time to time. Scrape off salt and dill.

3 Gravlax will keep in the refrigerator for about a week.

Serve with cold beer, aquavit, or California Sauvignon Blanc.

Wild Salmon Paillard Karine

Makes 4 servings

$2^{1}/_{2}$ pounds gravlax (see page 87)

$^{1}/_{2}$ cup Sweden sauce (see page 188)

$^{1}/_{2}$ cup hollandaise sauce (see page 181)

2 lemons, cut in half

Because all the components for this recipe can be made in advance, the cook will spend very little time in the final preparation when company comes. My daughter Karine is enamored of this dish. Salmon trout can also be used in this recipe. (Photo 2 following page 82.)

1 Preheat the barbecue. Cut the salmon into 4 pieces. Place on oiled barbecue rack and grill for 3 minutes on each side.

2 In a small saucepan combine Sweden sauce with hollandaise sauce and heat gently. Pour into sauceboat. Place a lemon half on each plate alongside the salmon and spoon sauce over the fish.

Serve with chilled beer or Muscadet.

Grilled Salmon Danish Style

The original feature of this fantastic dish is that it cooks from the bottom and is never touched. The Danes say this is the best way to cook salmon; the scales protect the skin and the skin protects the meat. Accompany the fish with baked potatoes topped with sour cream and chives. Salmon trout can also be used in this recipe.

Makes 4 servings

4 salmon fillets (6 to 7 ounces each), skin on
1 tablespoon coarse kosher salt
2 tablespoons water
2 tablespoons aquavit
1 cup (2 sticks) unsalted butter
salt and freshly ground black pepper
2 tablespoons chopped fresh dill
4 sprigs fresh dill

1 Prepare barbecue grill. When coal is glowing, place fish on grill rack and sprinkle with salt. Cook for 10 minutes without touching the fish.

2 In a saucepan, bring water and aquavit to a boil. Whisk in the butter a tablespoon at a time; continue whisking until thick. Season to taste with salt and pepper and add the chopped dill. Place each fillet in the center of a heated plate and decorate with a sprig of dill. Serve sauce in a sauceboat.

Serve chilled Danish beer or California Sauvignon Blanc.

Minced Salmon Wilfried

This is named after my son Wilfried because it is his favorite salmon dish. Well worth the extra effort and expense, it makes a richly satisfying centerpiece for an important dinner. Salmon trout can also be used in this recipe.

Makes 4 servings

1 cup half and half or light cream

3 tablespoons unsalted butter

½ cup water

salt and freshly ground white pepper

2 pounds fresh salmon fillets

2 artichoke bottoms, sliced into 3 rounds, then each round quartered

1 pound medium mushrooms, sliced

¼ pound morels, cleaned very thoroughly, or 1 ounce dried morels, soaked for 10 minutes and rinsed well

3 tablespoons heavy cream

1 teaspoon beef stock base or ¼ beef bouillon cube

2 tablespoons Cognac or other brandy

5 tablespoons hollandaise sauce (see page 181)

1 Preheat oven to 475°F. In a large skillet heat the half and half, 2 tablespoons of the butter, water, salt and pepper. Cut fillets into 4 pieces and poach in the half and half mixture for 7 minutes. Set aside and keep warm.

2 Sauté artichoke bottoms and mushrooms in remaining 1 tablespoon butter over high heat until all liquid has evaporated. Keep warm.

3 In a small saucepan combine morels, heavy cream and beef base and simmer for 5 minutes. Remove morels and set aside; reserve the cream mixture.

4 Arrange the artichoke mixture and the morels on a large ovenproof platter. Arrange the fish over the vegetables.

5 Reheat the morel sauce, whisking in Cognac and hollandaise. Spoon over the fish. Place in the preheated oven for 3 minutes or until lightly browned. Serve immediately.

Wine—Meursault or Chenin Blanc, served chilled.

Skate with Almonds

The names skate and ray are used interchangeably. Although they are not of the same species, both have flat bodies and long, thin tails and are found throughout the world. The fine quality of the edible part of the skate, its wings, is largely due to the consumption of mollusks. (Because of their texture, skate wings, cut into disks, have often been used as a substitute for scallops.) Before cooking, it's best to soak skate wings in a solution of 2 tablespoons distilled white vinegar and 1 quart water for about 2 hours. Serve this dish with small baked potatoes.

Makes 4 servings

2 pounds skinless skate wings
salt
5 tablespoons virgin olive oil
3 tablespoons fresh breadcrumbs
1 teaspoon chopped fresh parsley
16 blanched almonds
1½ pounds onions, sliced
3 cloves garlic
1 pound ripe tomatoes, peeled, seeded and chopped
pinch of saffron
freshly ground white pepper

1 Preheat oven to 350°F. Place fish in a shallow baking pan and sprinkle with salt.

2 Heat 2 tablespoons oil in a skillet over medium heat. Add breadcrumbs, parsley and almonds and sauté until golden. Remove from skillet and grind in a blender or food processor.

3 Heat remaining 3 tablespoons oil in a skillet over high heat. Add onions, garlic, tomatoes, saffron, salt and pepper and cook for 10 minutes. Stir in breadcrumb mixture and spread over fish.

4 Bake for 10 minutes. Transfer fish to a heated platter. Over high heat, reduce liquid in baking pan to half its volume. Spoon over fish and serve.

Wine—Sancerre or California Chardonnay, served chilled.

Cold Skate and Tomato

Makes 4 servings

3 pounds skate wings
2 cups white wine vinegar
1 lemon, sliced
salt and freshly ground white pepper
1 cup olive oil
2 cloves garlic, minced
$1^{1}/_{2}$ pounds ripe tomatoes, peeled, seeded and chopped
2 sprigs fresh thyme (or $^{1}/_{8}$ teaspoon dried)

A fine warm-weather dish. Rice salad is a perfect accompaniment. Pompano can also be used in this recipe.

1 Wash fish and cut into serving-size pieces. Place in a nonaluminum pot with vinegar, lemon, salt and pepper and bring to a simmer. Poach for 20 minutes. Drain fish and discard skin and bones. Place on a serving platter.

2 While the fish is poaching, heat olive oil in a skillet over medium heat. Add garlic and cook until golden. Add tomatoes and season with salt, pepper and thyme. Cook gently for 25 minutes, then pour over the fish. Cover and chill. Serve cold.

Wine—Aligoté or California Chenin Blanc, served chilled.

Skate with Spinach and Pink Grapefruit Salad

When we have skate, we are actually eating the wing, which is the edible portion. Skate wings are generally marketed with the skin left on, although it is possible to buy them skinned. One of the pluses of the skate wing is that it has no tiny bones to deal with. The flesh has excellent flavor and is considered a delicacy in Europe. This makes a lovely summertime salad. Swordfish can also be used in this recipe.

Makes 4 servings

4 skate wings (1¼ pounds each)
court bouillon with milk (see page 166)
juice of 1 grapefruit
4 tablespoons unsalted butter
salt and freshly ground black pepper
1 pound fresh spinach, washed, dried and heavy stems removed
3 pink grapefruit, peeled and divided into sections

1 Place the skate in boiling salted water for 3 minutes. Remove and peel the skin off when cool enough to handle.

2 In a large nonaluminum pot, bring court bouillon to a boil. Add the skate wings and simmer for 10 minutes. Gently remove fish from liquid. Remove fillets from the central bone with a spatula. Trim to neaten. Place on a lightly buttered baking sheet and keep warm.

3 Bring the grapefruit juice to a boil in a nonaluminum saucepan. Whisk in the butter 1 tablespoon at a time. Season to taste with salt and pepper. Make a bed of spinach on each of 4 plates. Place a fillet of skate over the spinach and top with a crown of grapefruit segments. Spoon on the sauce and serve.

Wine—Bellet Rosé or California Grenache Rosé, served chilled.

Ceviche of Fish

Makes 4 servings

2 pounds fish fillets (sea bass, red snapper or grouper)

juice of 6 limes

2 onions, sliced and separated into rings

4 tomatoes, peeled, seeded and diced

1 sweet green pepper, cut into 1/2-inch dice

1 sweet red pepper, cut into 1/2-inch dice

salt and cayenne pepper to taste

2 tablespoons Niçoise olives

A wonderfully refreshing summer dish, the fish is "cooked" in a lime juice marinade. *(Photo 3 following page 82.)*

1 Cut fish fillets into 2-inch squares. Place in a glass dish and pour lime juice over. Marinate for 4 hours in refrigerator, turning fish 2 or 3 times.

2 Combine with onion rings, diced tomatoes and peppers. Season with salt and cayenne. Stir in olives. Serve chilled.

Wine—Macon Viré or Napa Valley Sauvignon Blanc, served chilled.

Red Snapper Baked Alaska

Our old friend turns up, not as a confection but as a hearty main dish. Serve it with rice cooked in fish fumet (see page 169). Pompano can also be used with this recipe.

Makes 4 servings

2 tablespoons unsalted butter
2 red snapper fillets (1 pound each)
salt and freshly ground white pepper
4 egg whites
2 tablespoons chopped fresh parsley
1 tablespoon chopped green peppercorns preserved in brine
1 tablespoon Dijon-style mustard
3 tablespoons fresh breadcrumbs
1/2 cup mustard sauce (see page 185)

1 Preheat oven to 375°F. Spread a baking pan with the butter. Place fish in pan and sprinkle with salt and pepper. Bake for 12 minutes, or until fish is opaque.

2 Meanwhile, beat egg whites until stiff but not dry. Fold in parsley, peppercorns and mustard. Spread mixture in a 1-inch layer over the fish and sprinkle with breadcrumbs. Bake for 6 more minutes. Serve with mustard sauce.

Wine—Chablis or California Sauvignon Blanc, served chilled.

Red Snapper with Fennel and Dill

Makes 4 servings

2 fennel bulbs, thinly sliced lengthwise

1 large stalk celery, julienned

$^{1}/_{3}$ cup olive oil

1 teaspoon paprika

cayenne pepper

1 large tomato, peeled, seeded and diced

4 Niçoise olives, pitted and diced

3 tablespoons chopped fresh parsley

4 red snapper fillets (7 ounces each)

salt and freshly ground black pepper

$^{1}/_{3}$ cup dry vermouth

$^{1}/_{3}$ cup dry white wine

1 bunch fresh dill (leaves only), chopped

Cayenne pepper adds zest to this dish. Adjust the spiciness to taste by using more or less cayenne. The olive oil, black olives and fennel provide a touch of Provence. Monkfish can also be used in this recipe.

1 Preheat oven to 400°F. Blanch the fennel in a large saucepan of boiling water for 1 minute. Add the celery and blanch for 1 minute longer. Drain.

2 In a small bowl, mix the olive oil, paprika and cayenne pepper to taste. Spoon $3^{1}/_{2}$ tablespoons of the seasoned olive oil into the bottom of an 8- to 12-inch baking dish; add the fennel, celery, tomato, olives and parsley.

3 Season the snapper fillets with salt and black pepper and arrange on top of the vegetables in the baking dish. Brush the fillets with the remaining seasoned olive oil. Sprinkle the vermouth and white wine over the fish. Bake for 15 minutes.

4 To serve: Place a snapper fillet on each of 4 plates and surround with vegetables. Sprinkle fillets with dill.

Wine—Pouilly Fuissé or California Sauvignon Blanc, served chilled.

Baked Grey Sole with Swiss Cheese

Sole fillets lend themselves to many cooking styles. This unusual combination of fish, vegetables and cheese fulfills all the requirements for a complete one-dish meal. Other flatfish fillets can also be used in this recipe.

Makes 4 servings

1 cup virgin olive oil
3 large baking potatoes, peeled and sliced 1/2 inch thick
1 large onion, coarsely chopped
1 bunch parsley, chopped
1 cup grated Emmenthaler cheese
2 large tomatoes, peeled and sliced
2 1/2 pounds grey sole fillets
salt and freshly ground white pepper
1 1/2 cups dry white wine

1 Preheat oven to 350°F. Cover the bottom of a nonaluminum (preferably enamel) 12-inch gratin dish with the oil. Arrange the potatoes in the dish and top with the onion, parsley, cheese and half the tomatoes.

2 Arrange the fish over the top and season with salt and pepper. Top with the remaining tomato. Add the wine and bake for 1 hour, uncovered.

Wine—Macon Viré or California Chenin Blanc, served chilled.

Goujonettes of Sole

Makes 4 servings

1 1/2 pounds sole fillets
2 medium Idaho potatoes
5 tablespoons clarified unsalted butter (see note, page 181)
1/2 pound medium mushrooms, sliced
4 artichoke bottoms, diced
juice of 2 lemons
1/2 cup all-purpose flour
salt and freshly ground white pepper
2 tablespoons chopped fresh parsley

These delicious bite-size morsels swimming in a bath of clear lemon-spiked butter are sure to please the most exacting gourmet. It is easy to see why this dish, created during Napoleon's reign, should be a part of the cook's permanent repertoire. (Photo opposite.)

1 Wash fish fillets and cut crosswise into finger-size strips; pat dry. Cut potatoes into julienne the same length as the fish.

2 In a skillet, melt 1 tablespoon butter over high heat and sauté the potatoes for 4 minutes. Remove and set aside. Add 1 tablespoon butter to the skillet and sauté the mushrooms and artichoke bottoms for 6 minutes. Add the juice of 1 lemon. Remove from heat and set aside.

3 Coat fish in flour seasoned with salt and pepper, shaking off excess. Melt 1 1/2 tablespoons butter in a large skillet over medium heat. When the butter is brown, add fish and sauté for about 5 minutes. Add mushrooms and artichokes and cook for an additional 3 minutes. Divide among 4 heated soup bowls.

4 Melt the remaining 1 1/2 tablespoons butter in the skillet. When the butter is brown, add the juice of 1 lemon and the chopped parsley. Spoon this sauce over the fish and serve immediately.

Wine—Blanc de Blancs or California Pinot, served chilled.

Opposite: Goujonettes of Sole (page 98).
Page following: Smoked Trout, Crystal (page 106).

Sole, Spinach and Salmon Westbury

Although the recipe suggests two sauces as a garnish for this dish, the white butter sauce will do very nicely on its own. Serve with steamed potatoes. (Photo opposite.)

Makes 4 servings

1/2 pound spinach, washed, heavy stems removed

8 sole fillets (1/4 pound each)

1/2 pound smoked salmon, thinly sliced

salt and freshly ground white pepper

1/4 cup dry white wine

1 cup white butter sauce (see page 179)

1 cup sauce Américaine (optional; see page 176)

1 Blanch spinach leaves in boiling water just until wilted. Drain and chill in cold water. Drain again and dry with paper towels. Divide spinach into 8 portions. Spread 1 portion on a flat surface, overlapping leaves as necessary to make a sheet that will contain 1 fish fillet.

2 Place a sole fillet on the spinach; top with a slice of smoked salmon. Roll into a sausage shape. Season with salt and pepper and sprinkle with white wine. Repeat with remaining spinach and fish.

3 Cut 8 pieces of plastic wrap, each about 12 inches long. Place a rolled fish fillet on each piece of plastic and roll into a cylinder. Tie both ends closed. Arrange on a steaming rack and steam over boiling water for 5 minutes.

4 To serve: Discard plastic wrap. Cut each roll in half crosswise. Spread sauces on heated plates. Arrange fish over the sauce.

Wine—Meursault or California Chardonnay, served chilled.

Opposite: Sole, Spinach and Salmon Westbury (page 99).
Page preceding: Tuna Sushi in Chive Cream Sauce (page 107).

Fillet of Lemon Sole with Leek and Sorrel

Makes 4 servings

---

1 tablespoon unsalted butter

2 leeks, white part only, julienned

3 carrots, julienned

1 small celeriac (celery root), julienned (about 1/4 pound)

2 pounds fillets of lemon sole, cut into 1/2-inch-wide crosswise strips

1 cup Alsatian Riesling

1 cup heavy cream

2 egg yolks

1 bunch sorrel, finely julienned

salt and freshly ground white pepper

Any sole, flounder or plaice available in the market can replace the lemon sole used in this recipe. Sorrel is said to "melt" because it tends to liquefy when heated, as it does here. Serve the dish with steamed potatoes.

1 Melt butter in a large skillet over high heat. Add leeks, carrots and celeriac and sauté until lightly browned. Reduce heat to medium, add the fish and wine and cook for 8 minutes. Strain the broth into a saucepan and set the fish and vegetables aside in a warm place.

2 Bring the broth to a boil; boil for 3 minutes. Add cream, whisk in egg yolks and cook until sauce is slightly thickened.

3 Add sorrel and stir until it liquefies, about 2 minutes. Season sauce with salt and pepper.

4 Spoon sauce over fish and vegetables. Serve hot.

Wine—Alsatian Riesling or California Dry Riesling, served chilled.

Lemon Sole with Rice and Hard-Cooked Eggs

Really a fish-and-rice pilaf with the unusual enhancements of fish fumet and bechamel sauce. Grey sole or plaice can also be used in this recipe.

Makes 4 servings

3 pounds skinless lemon sole fillets
5 tablespoons unsalted butter
salt and freshly ground white pepper
1 onion, chopped
2 cups long-grain rice
2 cups fish fumet (see page 169)
1/2 cup bechamel sauce
pinch of cayenne pepper
3 hard-cooked eggs, chopped

1 Cut fish into 1/2-inch dice. Melt 2 tablespoons butter in a large skillet over medium heat and sauté fish for 3 minutes. Season with salt and pepper. Remove from pan and set aside.

2 Add the onion, rice and fish fumet to the skillet and bring to boil. Cover, turn heat to low and cook for 17 minutes, or until liquid is absorbed.

3 Prepare a bechamel sauce. Gently stir in fish, bechamel sauce, cayenne and eggs. Transfer to a platter.

4 Heat remaining 3 tablespoons butter until light brown. Spoon on top of pilaf and serve.

Wine—Macon Viré or California Chenin Blanc, served chilled.

Sautéed Lemon Sole with Tapenade

Makes 4 servings

3 large eggplants
1/4 cup virgin olive oil
3 cloves garlic, peeled and halved
3 sprigs fresh thyme (or 1/4 teaspoon dried)
3 tablespoons pitted black oil-cured olives
4 anchovy fillets in olive oil
salt and freshly ground white pepper
4 lemon sole fillets (3/4 pound each)
juice of 1 lemon

Tapenade, the Provençal standby, here does yeoman service as a sauce. Usually it is spread on toast or croutons, or used as a dip for raw vegetables.

1 Preheat oven to 350°F. Cut eggplants in half lengthwise and drizzle some of the oil over the cut sides. Place in a pan and bake for 20 minutes, or until soft.

2 Scoop meat out of eggplant and place in food processor with garlic, thyme, olives and anchovies. Process for 1 minute. Add salt and white pepper to taste and process tapenade for 1 more minute.

3 Heat remaining oil in a skillet over medium heat. Add fish and sauté for about 4 minutes on each side, or until opaque.

4 Place the tapenade on a platter. Arrange fish on top, sprinkle with lemon juice and serve.

Wine—Blanc de Blancs de Provence or California Chenin Blanc, served chilled.

Lemon Sole with Gin Boulogne

Gin, a rarely used ingredient in French cooking, imparts subtle flavor to this dish. Other flatfish fillets can also be used in this recipe.

Makes 4 servings

2 tablespoons unsalted butter
8 fillets of sole (1/2 pound each)
salt and freshly ground white pepper
3 tablespoons virgin olive oil
1 onion, chopped
2 tablespoons all-purpose flour
3 tablespoons gin
1/2 cup water
1 cup minced mushrooms
1/2 cup fresh breadcrumbs

1 Preheat oven to 425°F. Spread a shallow baking pan with the butter. Sprinkle fillets with salt and pepper. Roll up into cylinders starting from the narrow end. Arrange in the baking pan.

2 Heat olive oil in a skillet over medium heat. Add onion and sauté until golden. Stir in flour.

3 Combine gin with 1/2 cup water, salt and pepper in a medium saucepan. Add mushrooms and cook over medium heat for 5 minutes. Spoon mixture on top of fish and bake for 20 minutes, or until fish is opaque. Sprinkle with breadcrumbs and bake 5 minutes more. Serve hot.

Wine—Entre-Deux-Mers or Mendocino County French Colombard, served chilled.

Fresh Sturgeon Grand'mère

Makes 4 servings

4 shallots, chopped
1 bunch chervil
1 bunch chives
3 sprigs fresh tarragon (or 1/4 teaspoon dried)
3 pounds sturgeon, cut into 1-inch-thick slices
1/2 cup California Chenin Blanc
salt and freshly ground white pepper
4 tablespoons unsalted butter
2 tablespoons all-purpose flour
1/2 cup boiling milk
1/2 cup boiling heavy cream

Sturgeon is relatively scarce but halibut or turbot makes a superb replacement. Serve with rice.

1 Preheat oven to 350°F. Butter a shallow baking pan and sprinkle with the shallots and herbs. Arrange fish in the pan and add wine, salt and pepper. Cover the pan with aluminum foil and bake for 25 minutes or until the fish flakes easily.

2 Meanwhile, prepare a bechamel sauce: Melt butter in a saucepan over low heat. Whisk in flour and cook slowly, whisking constantly, for 2 minutes; do not let mixture color. Whisk in the hot milk and cream. Increase heat to medium and stir until the sauce thickens.

3 Transfer fish to a warm platter. Whisk cooking juices into bechamel sauce over medium heat. Pour over fish and serve hot.

Wine—Muscadet or California Chenin Blanc, served chilled.

Grilled Swordfish with Horseradish Sauce

The sweet-hot sauce lends excitement to this dish; undercooking the fish makes it really succulent. Serve with fresh corn. Tuna can also be used in this recipe.

Makes 4 servings

4 center-cut swordfish steaks (7 ounces each)

1 tablespoon unsalted butter, melted

salt and freshly ground black pepper

1 cup heavy cream

2 tablespoons sherry vinegar

3 tablespoons horseradish, prepared or freshly grated

1 drop Tabasco sauce

1 Prepare barbecue grill. Brush both sides of each steak with melted butter; sprinkle with salt and pepper to taste. When coals are glowing, grill for 3 minutes on each side, undercooking the fish slightly. Remove and keep warm.

2 In a small nonaluminum saucepan, combine cream and vinegar. Cook over high heat for 5 minutes. Add horseradish and Tabasco; season to taste with salt. Place swordfish steaks in center of heated plates and surround with sauce.

Wine—Dry Rosé de Provence or California French Colombard, served chilled.

Smoked Trout, Crystal

Makes 4 servings

20 large asparagus, peeled and tough parts of stalk removed

8 eggs

salt and freshly ground white pepper

4 tablespoons cold unsalted butter

4 smoked trout fillets (3 ounces each)

1/4 cup hollandaise sauce (see page 181)

1 carrot, peeled and julienned

1 white icicle radish, peeled and julienned

1 cucumber, peeled and julienned

The crystal-like appearance of the vegetable garnish gives this dish its name. It is perfect for brunch. Smoked salmon or haddock can also be used in this recipe. (Photo 2 following page 98.)

1 Heat 4 plates in a warm oven.

2 Bring a large pot of salted water to boil. Plunge asparagus into the boiling water and cook for 12 minutes. Drain, rinse in cold water and pat dry.

3 In a mixing bowl, beat eggs with salt and pepper, melt 2 tablespoons butter in a saucepan over medium-low heat. When the butter has melted, add the eggs and whisk until they are scrambled. Add 2 tablespoons cold butter to the eggs to stop the cooking.

4 To serve: Place scrambled eggs in center of each warmed plate. Place smoked trout on one side, asparagus on the other side. Spoon on hollandaise sauce and trim the rim of the plate with julienned vegetables.

Wine—Alsatian Riesling or California Chenin Blanc, served chilled.

Tuna Sushi in Chive Cream Sauce

Tuna is probably the best-known sushi in this part of the world because it is abundant and available very fresh. The varicolored vegetables make an attractive garnish. Accompany with rye bread and butter. Halibut can also be used in this recipe. *(Photo 3 following page 98.)*

Makes 4 servings

1 small carrot, peeled and very finely julienned

1 small cucumber, peeled and very finely julienned

1 small red radish, very finely julienned

1 1/2 pounds extremely fresh red tuna fillet

3 tablespoons virgin olive oil

juice of 2 limes

3 sprigs fresh rosemary (or 1/2 teaspoon dried)

salt and freshly ground white pepper

1/2 cup heavy cream

2 tablespoons Sherry vinegar

3 tablespoons chopped fresh chives

1 Place the julienned vegetables into a large bowl of ice water for 1 hour. Cut tuna into very thin slices. Combine the olive oil, lime juice and rosemary in a non-aluminum bowl. Add tuna and marinate for 1 hour. Remove tuna from marinade and season with salt and pepper. Place on a cold platter and refrigerate.

2 Whip the cream to soft peaks. Add vinegar and chives and season with salt and pepper.

3 Place a spoonful of sauce in the center of 4 chilled plates. Arrange the tuna on top of the sauce. Drain the julienned vegetables and arrange around the tuna.

Wine—Provençal white, Bellet Crémant or California Sauvignon Blanc, served chilled.

Tuna Poached in Cream

Tuna belongs to the mackerel family. Bluefin and big eye are the redder varieties that we usually get in the market, but they are all interchangeable. A few seconds can make the difference between perfect cooking or overcooked tuna that tastes like canned. Swordfish can also be used in this recipe.

Makes 4 servings

2 cups heavy cream

4 center-cut red tuna steaks (7 ounces each), 1/2 inch thick

1 bay leaf

1 sprig fresh thyme (or 1/8 teaspoon dried)

salt and freshly ground black pepper

3 tablespoons pureed cooked potato, or 3 tablespoons dried potato flakes

optional vegetables: sautéed mushrooms or steamed carrots, turnips, zucchini or tomatoes

1 Combine the cream, tuna, bay leaf, thyme, salt and pepper in a heavy saucepan. Cook at a simmer for 7 minutes. Remove the fish with a slotted spoon and keep warm. Reduce the cream by boiling for 5 minutes. Strain into another saucepan and return to a boil. Add the potato puree, whisking until blended. Adjust seasoning with salt and pepper.

2 Add any of the optional vegetables and spoon over the tuna. Serve immediately.

Wine—Muscadet or California Chenin Blanc, served chilled.

Grilled Tuna Maquis

The Corsican maquis *are areas of wild, bushy land covering two-thirds of the island. This recipe's unusual treatment of grilling, then marinating and simmering produces an intense flavor. Serve the dish with rice. Swordfish can also be used in this recipe.*

1 Heat charcoal grill. When coals are glowing, place fish on an oiled rack and grill for 4 minutes on each side. Combine anchovies, lemon juice, olive oil, onions, garlic, thyme, bay leaf and basil. Add fish and marinate for 2 hours.

2 Transfer the fish and marinade to a large nonaluminum saucepan or Dutch oven and simmer gently for 30 minutes. Add tomatoes, wine and fish fumet and continue to cook over low heat for 1 hour. Season to taste with salt and pepper.

Wine—Macon Viré or California Chardonnay, served chilled.

Makes 4 servings

2½ pounds center-cut tuna steaks

6 anchovy fillets in olive oil, chopped

juice of 2 lemons

3 tablespoons virgin olive oil

3 onions, chopped

4 cloves garlic, chopped

2 sprigs fresh thyme (or ⅛ teaspoon dried)

1 bay leaf

6 basil leaves, julienned

1 pound ripe tomatoes, peeled, seeded and diced

2 cups California Chardonnay

1 cup fish fumet *(see page 169)*

salt and freshly ground white pepper

Medallions of Turbot with Apple

Makes 4 servings

4 turbot fillets (6 ounces each)

2 cups hard cider

1 cup fish fumet (see page 169)

1 cup heavy cream

1 cup (2 sticks) unsalted butter, at room temperature

salt and freshly ground white pepper

2 Golden Delicious apples, peeled, cored and julienned

4 Golden Delicious apples, unpeeled, halved crosswise and cored

1/4 cup tightly packed light brown sugar

2 tomatoes, peeled, seeded and chopped

1 bunch chervil or parsley, chopped

A member of the flounder family, turbot can grow to 30 pounds, although those found in the market are considerably smaller. Sole or brill are good substitutes for turbot. (Photo opposite page 19.)

1 Preheat broiler. Place a rack in the bottom of a large pot that will be able to accommodate a platter. Pour water into the pot to 1/2 inch below the rack. Arrange the fish in a single layer on a platter. Place on rack and turn heat to high. When water comes to a boil, cover the pot and steam fish for 4 minutes. Uncover the pot and remove platter.

2 Combine cider and fish fumet in a large nonaluminum saucepan. Bring to a boil and cook until the liquid is reduced by 2/3. Add the cream and reduce again by half. Whisk in the butter a tablespoon at a time. Whisking constantly, season with salt and pepper and add the julienned apples.

3 Place the apple halves on a buttered broiler pan. Sprinkle with brown sugar and broil until apples are glazed. Place a fish fillet on each plate and an apple half alongside. Nap with sauce and garnish with tomatoes and chervil.

Wine—French Chablis or California Chenin Blanc, served chilled.

Shellfish, Octopus and Squid

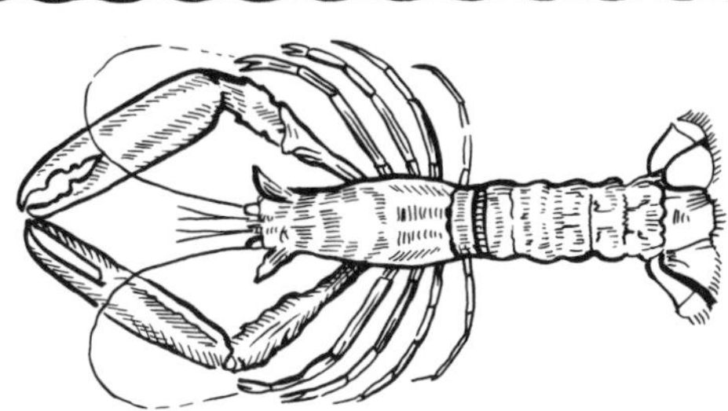

Madison Avenue Stuffed Clams

Makes 4 servings

4 tablespoons unsalted butter, melted
1 tablespoon chopped shallot
2 cloves garlic, chopped
2 cups dry breadcrumbs
finely grated zest of 2 limes
2 teaspoons Cognac
5 ounces lean ground beef
1 tablespoon chopped fresh parsley
2 teaspoons chopped fresh thyme
salt and freshly ground white pepper
24 cherrystone clams on the half shell

Nothing equals the taste of a fresh clam cooked to perfection. This recipe can be prepared hours ahead and cooked just before serving. (Photo 2 following page 18.)

1 Preheat broiler to high. Combine the melted butter, shallots, garlic, breadcrumbs, lime zest, Cognac, ground beef, parsley and thyme. Season to taste with salt and pepper and mix thoroughly. Top each clam with about 1 rounded teaspoon of the meat mixture.

2 Arrange the shells in a shallow baking dish. Place under the broiler for about 8 minutes, or until nicely browned on top.

Wine—French Chablis or California Sauvignon Blanc, served chilled.

Crab with Fennel

Blue crabs are the most common type found on the East Coast. The shells—that is, the top of the crab—can be saved. In this recipe, the top shell is stuffed. If thoroughly washed and dried, the shells can be stuffed again with purchased crabmeat; substitute bottled clam juice for the crab broth.

1 Melt butter in a large pot over high heat. Add carrot, leek, celery, shallots, wine, water, salt and pepper and bring to a boil. Add crabs, cover and boil for 5 minutes.

2 Remove crabs from broth. Remove meat from body and large claws; keep warm. Reserve the upper shells.

3 Boil the broth until reduced to 1 cup. Add tomatoes, Cognac and cream and boil for 7 minutes longer.

4 Meanwhile, boil the fennel in salted water until tender, about 10 minutes. Drain and cut into 1/8-inch dice.

5 Combine fennel with sauce and crabmeat and spoon into crab shells. Serve hot.

Wine—Alsatian Riesling or California Chenin Blanc, served chilled.

Makes 4 servings

2 tablespoons unsalted butter

1 carrot, cut into 1/8-inch dice

1 leek, cut into 1/8-inch dice

2 stalks celery, cut into 1/8-inch dice

2 shallots, chopped

1 cup dry white wine

1 cup water

salt and freshly ground white pepper

4 large or 8 small hard-shell blue crabs

3 tomatoes, peeled, seeded and diced

3 tablespoons Cognac

1 cup heavy cream

2 fennel bulbs

Crab Caribbean

Makes 4 servings

2 quarts court bouillon with white wine (see page 167)

8 hard-shell crabs, or ½ pound lump crabmeat

2 tablespoons olive oil

2 onions, chopped

2 garlic cloves, chopped

4 shallots, chopped

1 bunch parsley, chopped

2 sprigs fresh thyme (or a pinch of dried)

1 bay leaf

½ cup fresh breadcrumbs

3 tablespoons milk

1 small hot red pepper, seeded and minced

salt and freshly ground white pepper

The "beautiful swimmers" are here given a tantalizing Caribbean treatment. Lump crabmeat can be substituted and the mixture baked in large scallop shells. (Photo opposite.)

1 Bring court bouillon to a boil and drop in the crabs. Poach for 12 minutes. Cool crabs in liquid. When cool enough to handle, remove meat from body and claws. Set aside meat and top shells.

2 Heat olive oil in a skillet over high heat. Add onions, garlic and shallots and cook for 10 minutes. Stir in parsley, thyme and bay leaf.

3 Meanwhile, combine breadcrumbs, milk, red pepper, salt and white pepper. Stir into vegetables in the skillet with crabmeat and cook gently for 7 minutes, stirring occasionally.

4 Fill reserved crab shells and serve.

Wine—Pouilly Fuissé or California Chenin Blanc, served chilled.

Opposite: Crab Caribbean (page 114).
Page following: Crayfish with Citrus Vinaigrette (page 118).

Soft-Shell Crabs in Two Blankets

A blanket of tomatoes and another of garlic, parsley and breadcrumbs enfold the crabs in nicely complementary flavors. Serve this dish with rice.

Makes 4 servings

8 soft-shell crabs
1/2 cup all-purpose flour
6 tablespoons unsalted butter
salt and freshly ground white pepper
3 tablespoons olive oil
4 tomatoes, peeled, seeded and chopped
2 sprigs thyme (or 1/8 teaspoon dried)
1 bay leaf
2 tablespoons chopped fresh parsley
3 tablespoons fresh breadcrumbs
5 cloves garlic, minced

1 If the crabs are not cleaned when purchased, wash and rinse them, then turn them on their backs and remove the "apron" in front. Pat dry with paper towels. Coat lightly with flour. Melt 3 tablespoons butter in a large skillet and sauté crabs over medium heat until lightly browned. Season to taste with salt and pepper. Remove from pan.

2 Heat oil in a nonaluminum saucepan over medium heat. Add tomatoes, thyme and bay leaf and simmer for 8 minutes. Pour onto a deep serving platter.

3 Arrange crabs over tomatoes. Combine parsley, breadcrumbs and garlic and sprinkle over crabs. Heat remaining 3 tablespoons butter until light brown and drizzle over crumb mixture. Serve immediately.

Wine—Provençal white or California Sauvignon Blanc, served chilled.

Opposite: Lobster Salad in Harlequin Dress (page 126).
Page preceding: Seafood Stew with Muscat Wine (page 120).

Soft-Shell Crabs Sautéed with Hazelnuts or Pecans

Makes 4 servings

8 medium-size soft-shell crabs

4 eggs

2 tablespoons milk

1 tablespoon Dijon-style mustard

salt and freshly ground black pepper

1 cup all-purpose flour

1 cup (2 sticks) unsalted butter

1/2 cup chopped hazelnuts or pecans

juice of 1 lemon

2 tablespoons chopped fresh parsley

Soft-shell crabs are blue crabs that have just shed their hard shells. Although they range from Delaware Bay to Florida, most are harvested from Chesapeake Bay. This dish is excellent served with steamed potatoes.

1 If the crabs are not cleaned when purchased, wash and rinse them, then turn them on their backs and remove the "apron" in front. Pat dry with paper towels.

2 Combine eggs, milk, mustard, salt and pepper. Dip the crabs in this mixture, then coat lightly with flour.

3 In a large skillet, heat 3 tablespoons butter over high heat until lightly browned. Add the crabs and sauté for 5 minutes on each side. Transfer to a heated platter and set aside in a warm oven.

4 In a saucepan, heat remaining butter until browned. Add the nuts and lemon juice. Spoon over the crabs and sprinkle with parsley.

Wine—Muscadet or New York State white, served chilled.

Witches' Pot

Crab claws always remind me of the fingers of Halloween witches, even though I usually serve the crabs outdoors in the summertime. This makes a rather messy meal but it's lots of fun, especially if each person is provided with a wooden board and mallet for cracking the shells.

1 Place crabs in a large kettle and add all remaining ingredients except the parsley. Bring to a boil and cook over high heat for 15 minutes.

2 Remove the crabs from the pot and divide them among 4 plates. Sprinkle with parsley and serve immediately.

Serve with chilled Aligoté wine or beer.

Makes 4 servings

- *8 to 12 Maryland hard-shell crabs, depending on size*
- *2 cups dry white wine*
- *1 cup dry vermouth*
- *1 onion, chopped*
- *3 cloves garlic with skin on, lightly crushed*
- *2 tablespoons tomato paste*
- *3 sprigs fresh thyme (or 1/4 teaspoon dried)*
- *2 bay leaves*
- *1 teaspoon ground coriander*
- *1 tablespoon chicken stock base or 1/2 bouillon cube*
- *1/4 cup chopped fresh parsley*

Crayfish Salad with Citrus Vinaigrette

Makes 4 servings

20 fresh crayfish

salt and freshly ground black pepper

$^1/_2$ pound fresh green beans

VINAIGRETTE

2 oranges, peeled and divided into sections

1 lemon, peeled and divided into sections

$^1/_2$ cup olive oil

5 fresh sage leaves (or 1 teaspoon dried)

$^1/_4$ teaspoon ground coriander

1 ripe tomato, peeled, seeded and chopped

salt and freshly ground white pepper

This delicious combination will appeal to the diet-conscious. Shrimp or langoustines can also be used in this recipe. (Photo 2 following page 114.)

1 Steam the crayfish for 8 minutes in a steamer or saucepan. Separate tail sections from the bodies of 16 of the crayfish. Remove and reserve the meat from the tails and discard shells and bodies. Reserve 4 whole crayfish to be used as decoration. Place the shelled crayfish tails in a baking dish. Season with salt and pepper and set aside.

2 Blanch the green beans in $1^1/_2$ quarts boiling salted water for 6 minutes. Cool immediately by plunging into ice water. Drain and set aside.

3 To prepare vinaigrette: Combine the orange and lemon sections, olive oil, sage and coriander in a food processor or blender and mix for a few seconds. Transfer to a small nonaluminum saucepan. Stir in the tomato and season with salt and pepper to taste. Set aside.

4 Preheat oven to 325°F. Arrange salad greens in the center of 4 plates. Place green beans on both sides of the salad and zucchini at the lower end of the plate.

5 Place the crayfish in the preheated oven for 3 minutes. Meanwhile, heat the vinaigrette on top of the stove.

6 To serve: Arrange the crayfish on top of the salad greens. Place 2 whole basil leaves and 2 cherry tomatoes on each side of the crayfish. Pour the vinaigrette over the salad and sprinkle with the basil strips. Place whole unshelled crayfish atop each salad to decorate.

Wine—Rosé de Provence or California Grenache Rosé, served chilled.

SALAD

1 bunch arugula, mâche, watercress or Boston-type lettuce

2 small zucchini, sliced into 2½-inch strips

16 basil leaves, 8 left whole and 8 cut into long, thin strips

8 cherry tomatoes

Seafood Stew with Muscat Wine

Makes 4 servings

16 live crayfish
1 small zucchini
1 medium carrot
1 medium turnip
3/4 cup muscat wine
1 2-inch piece fresh ginger, peeled and sliced
3 tablespoons heavy cream
12 tablespoons (1 1/2 sticks) cold unsalted butter
juice of 1/2 lime
salt and freshly ground white pepper
16 raw langoustines, shelled and deveined
grated zest of 1 lime
4 large sprigs fresh dill

The combination of crayfish and langoustines provides an interesting contrast between freshwater and saltwater shellfish. (Photo 3 following page 114.)

1 Bring 3 cups water to a boil. Add the crayfish and cook for 6 minutes. Drain and detach tail sections with a small knife.

2 Carve the zucchini, carrot and turnip into olive shapes. Blanch the vegetables separately in boiling salted water—the zucchini for 5 minutes, the turnip and carrot for 8 minutes. Refresh all the vegetables immediately under cold water. Drain and set aside.

3 Combine the wine and ginger in a small nonaluminum saucepan and simmer for about 25 minutes, or until the wine is reduced to 2 tablespoons. Add the cream and boil for 5 minutes or until reduced to 1 1/2 tablespoons. Off heat, whisk in the butter 1 tablespoon at a time. Add the lime juice and season with salt and pepper to taste. Set aside.

4 Preheat oven to 500°F. Place crayfish tails and langoustines in separate buttered baking dishes. Season with salt and pepper. Bake langoustine for 1 minute. Reheat crayfish in oven with the door open for 2 minutes. Reheat vegetables in a steamer set over boiling water, being careful not to overcook them. Return the sauce to the stove and place over low heat, whisking constantly, until warm. Strain.

5 To serve: Arrange crayfish, langoustines and vegetables attractively on 4 serving plates. Spoon the sauce over the seafood and sprinkle with the grated lime zest. Decorate each serving with a sprig of dill.

Wine—Muscat from Languedoc or
California Johannisberg Riesling, served chilled.

Haricots Verts Salad with Langoustines and Hazelnuts

Makes 4 servings

2 pounds haricots verts (tiny French green beans) or the smallest green beans available

1 carrot, peeled and sliced

1 small onion, sliced

1 stalk celery, sliced

1 bay leaf

1 sprig fresh thyme (or 1/4 teaspoon dried)

salt and freshly ground black pepper

24 very fresh langoustines or shrimp

1/4 cup red wine vinegar

1 teaspoon Dijon-style mustard

1 egg yolk

1/2 cup hazelnut oil

3 tablespoons chopped hazelnuts

1 tablespoon chopped fresh coriander

All shrimp are referred to as such in the States. In other places, large shrimp are known as prawns. Langoustines, also called Norway lobsters or Dublin Bay prawns, are neither—but they are delicious.

1 Drop the beans into a large pot of boiling salted water and boil for 6 minutes. Drain and cool in ice water. Drain again and set aside.

2 In a saucepan, combine carrot, onion, celery, bay leaf, thyme, salt and pepper with 2 quarts water. Bring to a boil, cover and cook for 15 minutes. Add langoustines, return to boil, and cook for exactly 3 minutes. Drain.

3 To prepare sauce by hand: Whisk together vinegar, mustard and yolk. Add oil 1 teaspoon at a time, whisking until thickened; then add oil more quickly as the sauce emulsifies. Season with salt and pepper.

To prepare sauce in a food processor or blender: Combine vinegar, mustard, egg yolk, salt and pepper. Process for about 15 seconds or until egg becomes fluffy. With machine running, pour oil through feed tube very slowly until mixture begins to thicken; then continue pouring a little more rapidly until all the oil is incorporated. Adjust seasoning to taste.

Toss sauce with green beans and transfer to a large platter; arrange langoustines on top, tails up. Sprinkle with hazelnuts and coriander.

Wine—Muscadet-sur-lie or California Johannisberg Riesling, served chilled.

Lobster Big Apple

Baked apple slices and lobster may seem an unusual combination, but they go together very well. This is one of the most often requested dishes at the Polo Restaurant.

1 Combine the olive oil and vegetables in a pot large enough to hold the lobsters. Cook the vegetables over medium heat just until they begin to color. Stir in the tarragon, thyme, bay leaves and garlic, then add the lobsters, Cognac, Port and Calvados. Increase heat to high, cover and cook for 12 minutes. Remove the lobsters from the pot and continue to cook the liquid until reduced to 1 cup. Gently stir in the cream and tomato paste. Season with salt and pepper and set aside.

2 Preheat oven to 400°F, or preheat broiler. Peel, core and slice the apples. Arrange them in a shallow roasting pan and bake or broil until lightly browned. Set aside.

3 To serve: Strain the sauce and reheat gently. Cut the lobsters in half lengthwise and arrange two halves on each plate. Top with apple slices and spoon the sauce around the lobsters.

Serve with very cold hard cider or chilled French Chablis.

Makes 4 servings

3 tablespoons virgin olive oil
1 carrot, peeled and diced
1 onion, peeled and diced
3 shallots, peeled and diced
2 stalks celery, diced
3 sprigs fresh tarragon (or 1/2 teaspoon dried)
3 sprigs fresh thyme (or 1/4 teaspoon dried)
2 bay leaves
2 cloves garlic, lightly crushed
4 live lobsters (1 1/2 pounds each)
1 cup Cognac
1 cup Port
2 cups Calvados or applejack
2 cups heavy cream
1 tablespoon tomato paste
salt and freshly ground black pepper
2 Golden Delicious apples

Joel's Barbecued Maine Lobster

Makes 4 servings

4 small live lobsters (1 pound each)

salt and freshly ground black pepper

2 tablespoons olive oil

2 tablespoons Pernod

4 tablespoons unsalted butter

3 tablespoons finely chopped fresh basil

Joel, a friend who is also a chef, cooks this for me. A barbecue is the best cooking method, but if none is available, bake the lobsters in the oven. Serve them with plain steamed rice. One-pound lobsters are usually referred to as chicken lobsters or "chicks."

1 Prepare barbecue grill until coals are glowing or preheat oven to 475°F. Cut lobsters in half lengthwise and remove sac between the eyes (this is the stomach). Break or cut off the claws and place them on a baking sheet. Bake in the oven for 10 minutes. Salt and pepper the lobster meat and brush with olive oil. Place meat side down on the grill for 3 minutes. Turn the meat side up and sprinkle the Pernod onto the lobster, being careful not to drop any onto the flames.

2 Melt the butter in a small saucepan, add the chopped basil and cook for 5 minutes. Serve lobster and claws and pass the butter sauce separately.

Wine—White Saint-Tropez or California Sauvignon Blanc, served chilled.

Warm Lobster Salad in Vermouth Butter

A colorful variety of ingredients and the cook's creativity make possible a very attractive presentation. The vegetables will, of course, vary with the season.

1 Place enough water to cover the lobsters in a kettle. Add 1 tablespoon salt, the bay leaf, thyme and peppercorns. Add the lobsters and, when the water returns to a boil, cook for 12 minutes. Remove the lobsters and set aside.

2 Blanch the beans and asparagus in separate pots of boiling water to cover for 6 minutes. Immediately cool by plunging into ice water. Drain and set aside.

3 Arrange the lettuce in the center of an ovenproof serving platter. Surround with the mushrooms and blanched vegetables, and arrange the fruit in a larger circle around the vegetables. Cut lobsters in half lengthwise and arrange over the lettuce, vegetables and fruit.

4 Bring the vermouth to boil in a nonaluminum saucepan; boil until reduced to 1/4 cup. Whisk in the butter 1 tablespoon at a time. Season to taste with pepper.

5 To serve: Preheat oven to 425°F. Heat the platter of lobster salad in the oven for 2 1/2 minutes. Cover with the vermouth butter. Sprinkle with chopped chervil or parsley and garnish each serving with a cherry tomato.

Wine—Pouilly Fumé or California Chardonnay, served chilled.

Makes 4 servings

1 tablespoon salt
1 bay leaf
1 large sprig fresh thyme (or 1 teaspoon dried)
12 black peppercorns
2 live Maine lobsters (1 1/2 pounds each)
1/2 pound smallest possible fresh string beans or haricots verts
4 stalks asparagus
1 head romaine lettuce, cut into thin strips
1/4 pound mushrooms, thinly sliced
1 grapefruit, and
2 oranges, peeled and cut into eighths
3/4 cup dry vermouth
1 cup (2 sticks) unsalted butter
freshly ground white pepper
minced fresh chervil or parsley
4 cherry tomatoes

Lobster Salad in Harlequin Dress

Makes 4 servings

1 carrot, sliced
1 onion, sliced
1 stalk celery, sliced
1 bouquet garni, 4 parsley sprigs, 1 bay leaf, 2 sprigs fresh thyme and 1 stalk celery
1/2 cup wine vinegar
15 peppercorns
1 teaspoon salt
4 live Maine lobsters (1 pound each)
Vinaigrette (see page 190)
2 ripe tomatoes, peeled, seeded and diced
Peel, seed and slice:
1 Golden Delicious apple
1 large avocado
1 papaya
1 mango
3 tablespoons (about) fresh lemon juice
4 teaspoons chopped fresh chives
4 teaspoons fresh chervil leaves

This recipe works equally well with langoustines or crayfish. (Photo opposite page 115.)

1 In a large stockpot, combine 3 quarts water, carrot, onion, celery, bouquet garni, vinegar, peppercorn, and salt. Bring to a boil, then reduce heat and simmer for 30 minutes. Strain liquid into another stockpot. Add lobsters and cook for 6 minutes once the liquid comes to a boil. Cool lobsters in the liquid.

2 When the lobsters are cool, separate tails from the bodies, crack claws, remove meat and refrigerate. Reserve carcasses for lobster bisque if desired.

3 To serve: Place about 3 tablespoons vinaigrette on each of 4 plates together with the diced tomato. Slice lobster tails into medallions and toss with the claw meat and the remaining vinaigrette. Place lobster meat in the center of each plate. As the fruit is sliced, coat it with lemon juice to prevent discoloration. Arrange fruit around the lobster, napping with the vinaigrette on the plate. Garnish with chives and chervil.

Wine—Muscadet de Sèvre-et-Maine or California French Colombard, served chilled.

Mussels Danielle

Mussels have long been prized in Europe and largely ignored here, but lately they are gaining in popularity and are no longer confined to ethnic menus. My wife, Danielle, prepares this recipe for our family. Salt is not added, as the mussels are sufficiently salty on their own. Steamer clams can also be used in this recipe.

Makes 4 servings

4 pounds mussels
1 cup dry white wine
12 shallots, chopped
12 sprigs fresh thyme (or 1 teaspoon dried)
3 bay leaves
1 sprig fresh rosemary (or 1/2 teaspoon dried)
1 cup heavy cream
3 large egg yolks
3 tablespoons coarse-grained mustard such as Pommery
freshly ground black pepper
1 teaspoon chopped fresh rosemary (or 1/2 teaspoon dried)

1 Scrub the mussels and debeard with a small knife. Soak in cold water for 1 hour to remove additional sand. Combine the wine, shallots, thyme, bay leaves and 1 sprig rosemary in a large stockpot. Add the mussels, cover and steam over high heat for 6 to 8 minutes, shaking the pot frequently so that mussels cook evenly. Discard any unopened mussels.

2 Remove the mussels from the broth and discard one shell from each. Strain the broth, return to the pot and boil over high heat until reduced by half.

3 Divide the mussels, on the half shell, among 4 soup bowls; keep warm. Combine the cream, egg yolks and mustard in a bowl and whisk into the hot reduced mussel broth; continue to boil and whisk for 3 minutes. Add pepper to taste with chopped rosemary. Ladle sauce over mussels and serve.

Wine—Muscadet-sur-lie or dry California Chablis, served chilled.

Mussels, Sailor Fashion (Moules Marinière)

Makes 4 servings

4 pounds mussels
1 onion, minced
1 bouquet garni, consisting of 6 parsley sprigs, 4 sprigs fresh thyme (or 1/4 teaspoon dried) and 1/2 bay leaf
1 cup water
2 tablespoons unsalted butter
2 tablespoons chopped fresh parsley
4 shallots, chopped
1 cup fresh breadcrumbs
juice of 1 lemon
salt and freshly ground white pepper

When steaming mussels, be sure to use a pot large enough to contain them when the shells spring open. Serving the mussels out of the shell makes for easy eating. Accompany with steamed potatoes. Steamer clams can also be used in this recipe.

1 Scrub the mussels and debeard with a small knife. Soak in cold water for 1 hour to remove sand.

2 Place mussels in a 6-quart pot with onion, bouquet garni and water. Turn heat to high and bring to a boil. Cover and cook for 4 minutes, shaking the pot from time to time.

3 Remove mussels from broth with a slotted spoon; reserve broth. Remove and discard mussel shells; discard any unopened mussels.

4 Melt butter in a large skillet over medium heat. Add mussels, parsley and shallots and sauté for 3 minutes, turning the mussels in the butter.

5 Strain 1 cup mussel broth through a double layer of cheesecloth and add to the skillet. Sprinkle with the breadcrumbs and lemon juice; season to taste with salt and pepper. Cook for an additional 2 minutes. Serve immediately.

Wine—Pouilly Fumé or California Sauvignon Blanc, served chilled.

Mussels and Squash in Cream Sauce

One is lucky to live near the seashore, where mussels grow in abundance and are there for the taking. But lacking that advantage, they are now easy to find in fishmarkets and supermarkets and they are very low in cost. Steamer clams can also be used in this recipe.

Makes 4 servings

$4^1/_2$ pounds small mussels
6 tablespoons virgin olive oil
8 whole cloves
1 bouquet garni, consisting of 2 parsley sprigs, $^1/_2$ bay leaf, 1 sprig fresh thyme (or $^1/_8$ teaspoon dried) and 1 stalk celery
2 zucchini, julienned
1 sweet red pepper, julienned
2 yellow squash, julienned
6 tablespoons water
salt and freshly ground white pepper
6 egg yolks
1 cup heavy cream
2 tablespoons chopped fresh parsley

1 Scrub the mussels and debeard with a small knife. Soak in cold water for 1 hour to remove additional sand. Place in a large stockpot with 4 tablespoons of the oil, the cloves and bouquet garni. Cover and cook over high heat for 5 minutes, shaking the pot frequently so that mussels cook evenly. Discard any unopened mussels.

2 Place the remaining 2 tablespoons oil in a skillet and add the vegetables, 6 tablespoons water, salt and pepper and cook over medium-high heat until all the water is evaporated. Remove mussels from the broth, open them and discard the empty half shell from each. Arrange the mussels in 4 deep plates or soup bowls. Top with the vegetables and keep warm.

3 Strain the mussel broth into a saucepan and bring to a boil. In a large mixing bowl, combine egg yolks and cream and whisk until lightly whipped or until a bit of cream dropped from the whisk will retain its shape. Whisk in the boiling broth. Return the mixture to the saucepan and boil for 2 minutes, whisking constantly. Pour sauce over the mussels and sprinkle with parsley. Serve hot.

Wine—Bellet Coteaux de Nice or California Rhine, served chilled.

Eight Arms with Rice

Makes 4 servings

1½ pounds octopus
3 tablespoons virgin olive oil
1 large onion, finely chopped
3 cloves garlic, chopped
3 tomatoes, peeled, seeded and diced
1 sprig fresh thyme (or ¼ teaspoon dried)
1 tablespoon chopped fresh parsley
1 cup dry white wine
1 cup parboiled rice
1 cup water
1 teaspoon tomato paste
salt and freshly ground black pepper

The octopus is a cephalopod, which means that the tentacles sprout from the head. Formerly found only in ethnic fishmarkets, it is now widely available. Squid can also be used in this recipe.

1 Remove and discard head and beak of octopus; rinse tentacles and slice into thick rings. Heat olive oil in a large saucepan and add onion, garlic, tomatoes and thyme. Cut a round of waxed paper to fit pan and place on the vegetables, covering them completely; then place lid on pan. Simmer over low heat for 10 minutes.

2 Add octopus, parsley and wine, cover and cook over medium heat for 25 minutes. Add rice, water and tomato paste; season to taste with salt and pepper and cook, covered, over low heat for an additional 25 minutes.

Wine—A light Italian red or California Merlot, served cool or at room temperature.

Opposite: Prawns Early Morning (page 142).
Page following: Bay Scallops with Pasta and Wild Mushrooms (page 137).

MARSEILLE
CUEILLETTE
EXTRA VIRGIN
16 FL OZ (1PT)

Belon Oysters in Sauce Sauternes

One need no longer travel to Brittany to eat a Belon oyster. For the past few years, they have been successfully cultivated in Maine. Belons are not essential to this dish; any good oyster will do. (Photo opposite.)

Makes 4 servings

24 fresh Belon oysters
3 shallots, very finely chopped
1/2 cup Sauternes
1 cup heavy cream
1 tablespoon unsalted butter
1 pound spinach, washed
4 large egg yolks
1/4 cup whipped cream

1 Preheat the grill or broiler. Shuck the oysters, reserving half the shells. Place oysters, together with their liquor, in a large nonaluminum saucepan. Add the shallots and wine.

2 Cook the oysters over medium heat for 3 minutes. Remove them from the pan with a slotted spoon and keep warm. Boil the liquid remaining in the pan until reduced to 2 tablespoons. Add the cream and boil until reduced to 1/2 cup.

3 In a pot large enough to hold the spinach, melt the butter. Add the spinach and sauté over high heat for 4 minutes. Drain.

4 Place 6 oyster shells in each of 4 gratin dishes. Divide the spinach evenly among the shells, pressing in lightly. Top each with an oyster and spoon the Sauternes sauce over.

5 Beat the egg yolks lightly and fold them into the whipped cream. Place a spoonful of the mixture on each oyster and broil until lightly browned. Serve immediately.

Wine—Sauternes or Johannesberg Riesling, served chilled.

Opposite: Belon Oysters in Sauce Sauternes (page 131).
Page preceding: Scallop and Smoked Duck Salad (page 140).

Shellfish Omelet Côte Opale

Makes 4 servings

1 pound mussels, scrubbed and debearded

1 pound littleneck clams

12 oysters

5 tablespoons virgin olive oil

1 clove garlic, chopped

1 pound shrimp in the shell

1/2 cup heavy cream

8 eggs

salt and freshly ground white pepper

5 tablespoons finely chopped fresh parsley

The southern shore of Brittany near La Baule, known as the Côte Opale *(Opal Coast), brings us this dish redolent of the sea. (Photo opposite page 179.)*

1 Preheat oven to 475°F. Arrange mussels, clams and oysters on a rimmed baking sheet and place in the oven for 2 minutes or just until the shells open. Remove from oven.

2 Remove meat from the shells over a bowl in order to catch the juices.

3 Heat 2 tablespoons olive oil in a large skillet over medium heat. Add garlic and cook just until slightly golden. Add shrimp, increase heat to high and sauté for 3 minutes. Remove from skillet and shell the shrimp.

4 Place reserved shellfish juices in a small saucepan and boil over high heat until reduced to 2 tablespoons. Add cream and boil for 3 minutes. Combine cream mixture with all the shellfish.

5 Beat eggs well with salt, pepper and parsley. Heat remaining 3 tablespoons oil in a large omelet pan or skillet. When the oil is sizzling, pour in the egg mixture. Stir gently as the omelet cooks.

6 When the eggs are partially cooked but still soft, spoon the seafood mixture across center of omelet. Flip near end of omelet over the filling and roll omelet to far side of pan. Turn omelet out onto a plate and serve.

Wine—Sancerre or California Sauvignon Blanc, served chilled.

Oysters Florida Fashion

Makes 4 servings

5 limes
3 pink grapefruit
4 oranges
24 oysters on the half shell, preferably Malpeque or Wellfleet
8 tablespoons (1 stick) unsalted butter
salt and cayenne pepper
seaweed (blanched for 2 minutes in boiling water and reserved in ice water), optional

Oysters lend themselves to a great variety of preparations. To some oyster lovers it is heresy to eat them any way but raw. We disagree, however, as evidenced by this interesting combination of oysters and citrus butter.

1 Peel and section the fruit over 3 separate bowls to catch the juices. Place a lime section on each of 8 oysters, a grapefruit section on 8 oysters, and an orange section on each of the remaining 8 oysters.

2 Place each remaining fruit and its juice into 3 separate small nonaluminum saucepans and heat over a medium flame. Divide butter into 3 equal parts and whisk one part into each saucepan; continue whisking until thick. The fruit sections will disintegrate as the sauce cooks. Season with salt and cayenne pepper.

3 Spoon the warm citrus butter over the oysters, each sauce corresponding to the fruit on the oysters.

4 Preheat the oven to 475°F. Bake oysters for 5 minutes. Decorate with blanched seaweed, if available from your fishmonger, and use under shells to hold shells in place. Serve immediately.

Wine—Cabernet Rosé, served chilled.

Blue Point Oysters and Clams with Green Herbs

Blue Points are just one of a great variety of oysters to be found on our shores. it is not usually possible to shop for a particular oyster on a given day; the oyster in the market on that day will, of necessity, be the oyster of choice.

Makes 4 servings

24 Blue Point oysters
48 littleneck clams
1 pound mixed greens and herbs, consisting of watercress, spinach, parsley, chervil and chives
1 cup (2 sticks) unsalted butter, at room temperature
salt and freshly ground black pepper
1/4 teaspoon anchovy paste
juice of 1/2 lemon
1/4 teaspoon minced garlic
1 drop Pernod or other nonsweet anise-flavor liquor
1 pound snow peas, cut into julienne
1 pound coarse kosher salt
2 firm-ripe tomatoes, peeled, seeded and chopped

1 Shuck oysters and clams, being careful to save all the liquor. Reserve half the shells. Combine the liquor, oysters and clams in a saucepan and simmer for 2 minutes. Pour the liquor through a fine strainer or a double thickness of cheesecloth.

2 Return liquor to a large saucepan and add the greens and herbs. When the watercress and spinach have wilted, whisk in the softened butter over medium heat 1 tablespoon at a time. Season with salt, pepper, anchovy paste, lemon juice, garlic and Pernod. Pass the mixture through a food mill.

3 Blanch snow peas in a large quantity of boiling salted water for 3 minutes. Plunge into cold water to stop the cooking process; drain well.

4 Make a bed of the salt on a large rimmed baking sheet. Arrange the oysters and clam shells on the salt. Divide the snow peas among all the shells and place either an oyster or a clam on each. Cover each with the green sauce.

5 Preheat oven to 450°F. Bake shellfish for 5 minutes. Garnish with chopped tomatoes and serve.

Wine—Sparkling Vouvray or California sparkling wine, served chilled.

Kabob of Sea Scallops with Garlic Butter

Makes 4 servings

$1^1/_2$ pounds sea scallops

2 teaspoons olive oil

2 sprigs fresh thyme (or $^1/_4$ teaspoon dried)

4 large bay leaves, broken into halves or thirds

bamboo skewers, soaked in water for 30 minutes or more

salt and freshly ground black pepper

6 tablespoons unsalted butter

10 cloves garlic, finely chopped

2 tablespoons finely chopped fresh parsley

The scallop is so named because of its scalloped shell, but most consumers never get to see the shells since they are removed as soon as the mollusks are harvested. Serve these easy-to-prepare kabobs with rice to soak up every drop of garlic butter. Monkfish can also be used in this recipe.

1 Wash scallops and pat dry. Place scallops in a mixing bowl and coat with olive oil and thyme.

2 Thread scallops and bay leaves alternately on bamboo skewers until skewers are full. Season with salt and pepper.

3 Preheat charcoal or gas grill. Barbecue kabobs for 2 minutes on each side, or just until scallops are opaque. Melt butter with garlic in a small saucepan and cook gently for 5 minutes. Season with salt and pepper to taste. Arrange kabobs on a platter, spoon on the garlic butter and sprinkle with parsley. Serve immediately.

Wine—Tavel Rosé or California Grenache Rosé, served chilled.

Bay Scallops with Pasta and Wild Mushrooms

Tiny bay scallops and shiitake mushrooms make this a truly special-occasion dish. Sea scallops can also be used in this recipe. *(Photo 2 following page 130.)*

Makes 4 servings

1 tablespoon olive oil
1 pound elbow macaroni
3 tablespoons unsalted butter
3 tablespoons finely chopped shallots
1½ pounds bay scallops, rinsed and dried
1 pound shiitake mushrooms, sliced
½ cup dry sherry
½ cup veal stock
½ cup heavy cream
3 tablespoons whipped cream
2 egg yolks

1 Bring 3 quarts salted water to boil with the olive oil. Add macaroni, return to the boil and cook for 9 minutes. Drain in a colander.

2 Heat a large skillet over medium heat, add butter and let it brown lightly. Add shallots and sauté until golden. Add scallops and mushrooms, increase heat to high and sauté for about 4 minutes or until scallops are opaque.

3 Remove scallops and mushrooms from skillet with a slotted spoon. Add sherry to the pan and scrape up browned bits with a spatula. Boil until only 2 tablespoons liquid remain. Add veal stock and cream and boil for 3 minutes.

4 Preheat broiler. Add pasta, scallops and mushrooms to the sauce and heat through. Divide among 4 soup bowls. Combine whipped cream and egg yolks and spoon over pasta mixture. Place under broiler for 15 seconds to glaze to a golden brown. Serve immediately.

Wine—Beaujolais or California Cabernet Sauvignon, served at room temperature.

Ravioli of Scallops

Makes 4 servings

1½ pounds sea scallops
1 teaspoon unsalted butter
⅓ cup crème fraîche
⅓ cup peeled, seeded and diced tomato
salt and cayenne pepper
40 wonton wrappers
50 fresh chervil leaves
1 large egg yolk, lightly beaten

The prospect of making pasta dough can discourage a cook, but the use of prepared wonton wrappers, made of the same noodle dough as ravioli, greatly facilitates the preparation of this filled pasta. The wrappers are now available in nearly all supermarkets. Each package contains about 90 to 100 pieces, which are thinner than most made at home. A cooperative fishmonger could save some lobster shells, which would make the preparation of the sauce quite inexpensive, yet luxurious. (Photo opposite page 178.)

1 Wash scallops and pat dry with a paper towel. Melt 1 teaspoon unsalted butter in a skillet over high heat. When the butter is brown, add the scallops and sauté for 2 minutes. Drain off excess liquid.

2 Combine ⅓ cup crème fraîche and diced tomato in a small bowl; season with salt and cayenne pepper.

3 Spread out 20 wonton skins on a work surface. Place one scallop on each skin. Top each with 1 teaspoon tomato mixture, then one chervil leaf.

4 Brush a ½-inch border of egg yolk on the remaining 20 wonton skins. Place them yolk side down on top of the scallops, pressing the edges together to seal tightly. Cut into 2½-inch circles using a cookie cutter. Seal edges together with the tines of a fork.

5 To prepare sauce: Heat olive oil in a heavy large saucepan over high heat. Add the lobster shells and carcasses and sauté for a few minutes. Add the vegetables and sauté until golden. Add wine, water and tomato paste, bring to a boil, cover and simmer 20 minutes. Strain the liquid, return to the saucepan and boil until reduced to 1¼ cups. Whisk in ½ cup crème fraîche and continue cooking and whisking for 5 minutes. Set aside.

6 To serve: Bring 3 quarts salted water to a boil. Add the ravioli, return to boil and cook 3 minutes. Drain in a colander. Reheat the sauce, whisk in 2 tablespoons butter and season with salt and cayenne pepper.

7 Place 5 ravioli in each of 4 heated dishes. Spoon the sauce around the ravioli and garnish with remaining chervil leaves.

Wine—White Châteauneuf-du-Pape or California Sauvignon Blanc, served chilled.

LOBSTER SAUCE

2 tablespoons olive oil

shells and carcasses of 2 lobsters

1 carrot, peeled and chopped

1 onion, peeled and chopped

1¼ cups dry white wine

1¼ cups water

2 tablespoons tomato paste

½ cup crème fraîche

2 tablespoons unsalted butter

Scallop and Smoked Duck Salad

Makes 4 servings

$^1/_2$ pound smoked duck breast, thinly sliced

16 sea scallops

assorted salad greens: radicchio, chicory, oakleaf lettuce, mâche, Bibb

hazelnut dressing (see below)

1 bunch chervil or parsley, chopped

HAZELNUT DRESSING

Makes about $^1/_4$ cup

1 teaspoon Dijon-style mustard

1 teaspoon red wine vinegar

salt and freshly ground white pepper

3 tablespoons hazelnut oil

Smoked duck breast is becoming easier to find in specialty food stores, and of course scallops are always at the fishmonger's. Although chervil, with its delicious anise flavor, is preferred as a garnish, parsley can be substituted. The assortment of salad greens depends on availability and personal preference. (Photo 3 following page 130.)

1 Wrap a slice of duck breast around each scallop and skewer with a toothpick. In an ungreased skillet, sauté over medium heat for 3 minutes on each side. (Smoked duck breast is fatty enough that no additional fat is needed.)

2 To prepare dressing: In a small bowl, whisk together mustard, vinegar, salt and white pepper. Slowly whisk in the oil, blending thoroughly.

3 Meanwhile, arrange greens on 4 plates. Sprinkle with hazelnut dressing. Arrange 4 scallop skewers over the greens on each plate. Garnish with chervil and serve.

Wine—Beaujolais or California Cabernet Sauvignon, served at room temperature.

Shrimp with Chive and Cinnamon Sauce

Cinnamon is the unusual ingredient in this butter sauce. Serve with steamed new potatoes. Sea scallops can also be used in this recipe. *(Photo opposite page 2.)*

Makes 4 servings

16 large shrimp, shelled and deveined
1 cup heavy cream
4 small green cabbage leaves

CHIVE SAUCE
2 tablespoons water
pinch of salt
1/2 teaspoon cinnamon
6 tablespoons cold unsalted butter
1 tablespoon soy sauce
2 tablespoons finely chopped fresh chives

3 cups vegetable oil
1 cup all-purpose flour
1 tablespoon butter
4 radishes, thinly sliced

1 Combine the shrimp and cream in a medium bowl; set aside. Blanch the cabbage leaves in boiling water for 2 to 3 minutes. Drain and cool in ice water. Drain again and set aside.

2 To prepare sauce: In a small saucepan, bring the water to boil with salt and cinnamon. Whisk in the 6 tablespoons butter 1 tablespoon at a time. Stir in the soy sauce and chives, remove from heat and keep warm.

3 Heat the oil to 360°F in a deep saucepan, wok or deep-fryer. Drain shrimp and coat with flour. Deep-fry for 2 minutes, cooking about 8 at a time to avoid cooling the oil too drastically. Drain on paper towels.

4 Melt 1 tablespoon butter in a saucepan. Add the cabbage and cook over high heat for 5 minutes, or until wilted but still green.

5 To serve: Place cabbage leaf in the center of each plate. Place 4 shrimp on each leaf and coat with the sauce. Sprinkle with radish slices.

Wine—Coteaux du Layon or California Johannesberg Riesling, served chilled.

Prawns Early Morning

Makes 4 servings

1½ pounds large shrimp
2 tablespoons unsalted butter
1 tablespoon chopped shallot
¼ cup dry white wine
1 teaspoon tomato paste
⅓ cup heavy cream
1 sprig fresh thyme (or ⅛ teaspoon dried)
salt and freshly ground white pepper
1 tablespoon chopped fresh parsley

The color resulting from the combination of heavy cream and tomato sauce recalls the early-morning sun. Serve with rice. Three dozen shucked littleneck clams can also be used in this recipe. (Photo opposite page 130.)

1 Shell, devein, rinse and dry shrimp. Heat butter in a large skillet over high heat until brown. Add the shrimp and sauté for 2 minutes on each side. Remove from the skillet and keep warm.

2 Add chopped shallot to skillet and sauté for 1 minute over high heat. Combine white wine, salt, pepper, parsley and tomato paste, add to skillet and cook over medium heat for about 5 minutes or until reduced to 1 tablespoon. Add the cream and thyme and boil for 3 minutes. Remove from heat and strain. Divide shrimp among 4 plates and spoon on sauce.

Wine—Alsatian Riesling or California Rhine, served chilled.

Shrimp Riviera

The aroma of this combination of herbs and fennel is the very essence of the Riviera. Sea scallops can also be used in this recipe. (Photo 2 following page 178.)

Makes 4 servings

3 tablespoons virgin olive oil

1 small head garlic, cut in half crosswise

2 sprigs fresh thyme (or 1/4 teaspoon dried)

2 bay leaves

1/2 fennel bulb, sliced lengthwise

2 pounds large shrimp, shelled

1/2 cup Cognac or other brandy

1 cup white butter sauce (see page 179)

juice and grated zest of 1 orange

salt and freshly ground white pepper

2 tablespoons finely chopped fresh basil

cooked rice

1 Heat olive oil in a large saucepan over high heat until smoking. Add garlic, thyme, bay leaves and fennel, stir and add shrimp and Cognac. Cover and remove from heat at once. Let stand for 3 to 4 minutes while heating the sauce.

2 In a small saucepan, heat the butter sauce with orange juice and zest. Season to taste with salt and pepper. Remove from heat and stir in chopped basil. Serve shrimp in deep bowls or soup dishes over rice. Top with sauce.

Wine—Rosé de Provence or Grenache Rosé, served chilled.

Shrimp with Sour Cream Blèsoise

Makes 4 servings

2 tablespoons unsalted butter

20 medium shrimp, shelled and deveined

1 tablespoon red wine vinegar

1 onion, chopped

1 tablespoon chopped fresh parsley

1 teaspoon fennel seed

1/2 cup fresh breadcrumbs

1/2 cup sour cream

2 tablespoons unsalted butter

salt and freshly ground white pepper

A Blèsoise is a woman from Blois, home of that famous château—and of my wife. This dish is typical of the region. Serve it with steamed rice. Sea scallops can also be used in this recipe.

1 Melt butter in a nonaluminum skillet over medium heat. Add shrimp and stir briefly. Add vinegar, onion, parsley and fennel seed and cook, covered, for 6 minutes.

2 Transfer shrimp to a platter. Boil liquid in skillet for 2 minutes. Stir in breadcrumbs and sour cream. Gradually stir in butter. Season to taste with salt and pepper. Spoon over shrimp and serve.

Wine—Sancerre or California Sauvignon Blanc, served chilled.

Squid Colin Maillard

The squid for this recipe must be fresh, not frozen, so that the ink sac contained in the body will be found when the head is removed. When the sacs of ink are cooked, the membranes containing the ink disappear.

Colin Maillard *is the French version of Blind Man's Buff. Its connection to this recipe is obscure, but one is free to speculate. Serve the dish with wild rice.*

Makes 4 servings

3 pounds fresh squid
3 tablespoons peanut oil
1 large onion, minced
2 tablespoons flour
4 cups Alsatian Sylvaner
salt and freshly ground white pepper
3 cloves garlic, minced
1 bunch parsley, chopped
1 hot red pepper

1 To clean squid, remove purplish skin and separate head and tentacles from the body. Separate tentacles from the head and discard the head. Remove and discard the transparent quill from the body; reserve ink sacs. Wash out the interior of the squid body. Cut squid body into 1-inch-wide rings; leave tentacles whole.

2 Heat oil in a Dutch oven over medium-low heat. Add onion and squid. Stir in flour. Add wine, salt and pepper and cook gently, covered, for 25 minutes.

3 Meanwhile, combine garlic, parsley, hot pepper and squid ink. Season to taste with salt and pepper. Add to squid and cook gently, covered, for 10 more minutes. Serve immediately.

Wine—Alsatian Sylvaner or California Sauvignon Blanc, served chilled.

Beer Batter Squid

Makes 4 servings

2 1/2 pounds squid
1 1/2 cups rye flour
1 tablespoon peanut oil
salt and freshly ground black pepper
2 cans or bottles of beer (12 ounces each)
5 egg whites, beaten until stiff but not dry
4 cups vegetable oil
2 bunches curly parsley

This is a superb appetizer. The combination of beer and rye flour imparts a tangy flavor to the batter. A word of caution: timing is critical in cooking squid. It must be cooked very briefly or for a long time, depending on the recipe; otherwise it will be tough. Here we cook the squid for 2 1/2 minutes. This recipe can also be prepared with smelts, whitebait or gudgeon. (Photo opposite.)

1 To clean squid, remove purplish skin and separate head and tentacles from the body. Separate tentacles from the head and discard the head. Remove and discard the transparent quill from the body. Wash out the interior of the squid body. Dry on paper towels. Cut squid body into 1/2-inch-wide rings; leave tentacles uncut.

2 In a mixing bowl, combine flour, 1 tablespoon peanut oil, salt and pepper and whisk to combine. Whisk in beer a little at a time. Carefully fold in the egg whites.

3 Heat oil in a deep-fryer to 375°F. Dip the squid rings and tentacles into the batter and fry in the deep fat for 2 1/2 minutes. Drain on paper towels. Keep warm.

4 Dry the parsley very well and plunge into the deep fat for 20 seconds. Drain on paper towels. Arrange the squid in a ring on a large platter and top with the parsley. Serve hot.

Serve with chilled beer, white wine or cocktails.

Opposite: Beer Batter Squid (page 146).
Page following: Pizza alla Porto Vecchio (page 152).

ROLLIN
ROCK
Premium Beer
ROLLIN
ROCK

Squid with Ham Bernadette

The squid, loved in the Far East and the Mediterranean, is now coming into its own in North America—and rightfully so. Eighty-percent-edible, 19-percent-protein squid lends itself to salads, sautéing, pan-frying or deep-frying. If the large squid called for are unavailable, use an equal weight of smaller squid. Serve with plain steamed rice.

Makes 4 servings

4 squid (9 ounces each)
1/4 pound smoked ham
3 ripe tomatoes, peeled and seeded
salt and freshly ground white pepper
1 teaspoon chopped fresh parsley
3 tablespoons olive oil
1 large onion, chopped
2 cloves garlic, chopped
2 sprigs fresh thyme (or 1/8 teaspoon dried)
1/2 cup dry rosé

1 To clean squid, remove purplish skin and separate head and tentacles from the body. Separate tentacles from the head and discard the head. Remove and discard the transparent quill from the body. Wash out the interior of the squid body.

2 Chop tentacles, ham and tomatoes. Combine with salt, pepper and parsley.

3 Preheat oven to 375°F. Stuff each squid with tomato mixture and skewer closed with a toothpick. Heat olive oil in a small skillet over medium heat. Reduce heat to low and add onion, garlic and thyme. Cover and cook for about 7 minutes or until soft and golden. Spoon mixture into a shallow baking pan.

4 Top with the squid and pour in the wine. Bake, covered, for 30 minutes. Serve hot.

Wine—Tavel Rosé or a California Cabernet Rosé, served chilled.

Opposite: Salmon with Sage in a Pastry Case (page 154).
Page preceding: Macaroni, Fennel and Sardine Pie (page 156).

Sea Urchins in a Spinach Nest

Makes 4 servings

12 sea urchins
1 pound fresh spinach, heavy stems removed
5 tablespoons cold unsalted butter
salt and freshly ground black pepper
fresh lemon juice

The sea urchin is an almost ball-shaped animal covered with green spines, which necessitate that it be held with a potholder or towel as it is cut open. The lid must be lifted in order to eat the roe, which is the edible part of the urchin. This is done by inserting scissors into the mouth—the concave part of the urchin—and then cutting a large circle which, in effect, becomes the lid.

1 As each urchin shell is opened, pour the juice into a small saucepan. Remove the roe with a small spoon and place in a bowl. Rinse the roe carefully and drain on a paper towel. Add the roe to the urchin juice in the saucepan. Wash spinach; drain but do not dry. Place in a large pot, cover and cook over high heat just until leaves are wilted, about 3 minutes (leaves should remain bright green). Drain in a colander. When slightly cooled, squeeze spinach between your hands at least 4 times to remove as much liquid as possible.

2 Melt 1 tablespoon butter in a sauté pan. Add the spinach and sauté over high heat until hot. Season with salt and pepper. Arrange in the center of 4 plates. Warm urchin roe in the liquid over low heat. Remove the roe from the juice with a slotted spoon and place 3 on each nest of spinach.

3 Bring the liquid in the saucepan to a boil. Remove from heat and whisk in the remaining 4 tablespoons butter. Season to taste with salt, pepper, and lemon juice. Spoon sauce over roe before serving.

Wine—Alsatian Sylvaner or California Sauvignon Blanc, served chilled.

Seafood Pies, Pastries and Terrines

Terrine of Black Bass and Asparagus

Makes 4 servings

8 asparagus tips
3/4 pound black bass fillets
salt and freshly ground white pepper
7 egg yolks, at room temperature
1 cup (2 sticks) unsalted butter, at room temperature
2/3 cup heavy cream
hollandaise sauce *(see page 181)*

The asparagus tops and hollandaise sauce enhance the presentation but do even more for the flavor of this terrine. Whiting can also be used in this recipe. *(Photo 2 following page 2.)*

1 Plunge asparagus into boiling salted water and cook for 8 minutes. Drain and rinse in ice water. Drain again and dry with paper towels. Reserve.

2 Combine fish with salt and pepper in a food processor and grind finely. Add egg yolks and process a few seconds. With machine running, add butter and cream; blend until very smooth.

3 Preheat oven to 350°F. Butter four 8-ounce soufflé molds or terrines. Spread a layer of fish mixture on the bottom of each. Place 2 asparagus tips on top and cover with another layer of fish.

4 Cover terrines with foil. Arrange them in a baking pan and add water to come halfway up the sides of the terrines. Bake for 7 minutes. Rotate terrines and bake for an additional 10 minutes; they will puff, then sink. Serve hot with hollandaise sauce.

Wine—Meursault or Sauvignon Blanc, served chilled.

Quiche of Crabmeat and Endive

This is my grandmother's recipe. She always made it for grandfather's birthday. Much to everyone's surprise, the quiche is made without a crust but forms its own when baked. It can be served as a canape, appetizer or main course. Shelled lobster or shrimp can also be used in this recipe. (Photo opposite page 18.)

1 In a large skillet, melt butter over high heat. Add endive, with salt and pepper to taste, and sauté for 4 minutes. Remove from pan and chill.

2 Preheat oven to 450°F. Butter a 9-inch pie plate or quiche pan *without* a removable bottom. Remove all bits of shell and cartilage and place crabmeat into the bottom of the pie plate. Add the endive. In a mixing bowl, beat eggs, flour, milk and a pinch of salt until well combined. Pour over the crabmeat and endive and bake for 35 minutes. Serve hot or warm.

Wine—Alsatian Riesling or California French Colombard, served chilled.

Makes 4 servings

2 tablespoons unsalted butter

3 Belgian endive, cleaned and minced

salt and freshly ground white pepper

1 cup fresh crabmeat

3 large eggs

3/4 cup all-purpose flour

2 cups milk

Pizza alla Porto Vecchio

Makes two 14-inch pizzas

2 tablespoons dry yeast

1¾ cups warm water

5 cups all-purpose flour

1 tablespoon salt

cornmeal

MUSSEL-GARLIC FILLING
2 pounds mussels or 2 dozen littleneck clams, steamed open, discard shells

6 cloves garlic, finely chopped

dried oregano or chopped fresh parsley

¾ cup olive oil

4 ripe tomatoes, peeled and sliced

SARDINE-OLIVE FILLING
2 pounds fresh sardines or other small whole fish, scaled and gutted

6 tomatoes, peeled, seeded and chopped

dried oregano

¾ cup olive oil

1 cup Niçoise olives

Corsican pizza reflects the influence of the sea. *(Photo 2 following page 146.)*

1 In a large bowl, dissolve yeast in 1 cup warm water together with a large pinch of flour. Mix well and allow to rest for 30 minutes.

2 Combine remaining water with salt and add to yeast mixture. Stir in remaining flour. Turn dough out on a floured surface and knead until smooth and elastic, about 10 minutes.

3 Return to the bowl, cover with plastic wrap and let rise in a warm place until doubled in bulk, about 2 hours.

4 Preheat oven to 475°F. Roll out dough into two 14-inch circles. Sprinkle cornmeal on a pizza pan or cookie sheet. Place rolled-out dough on top of the cornmeal. Top with ingredients for either filling, leaving a 1-inch border. Bake for 8 minutes, or until crust is golden brown. Serve immediately.

Wine—Chianti Classico or California Cabernet Sauvignon, served at room temperature.

Smoked Salmon Trout with Spinach in Puff Pastry

Smoked salmon trout, smoked trout, smoked salmon—any one of these can be used. (Photo 3 following page 2.)

Makes 4 servings

2 tablespoons unsalted butter

2 pounds fresh spinach, washed, heavy stems removed

salt and freshly ground white pepper

pinch of nutmeg

2 pounds puff pastry, commercial or homemade

1½ pounds smoked salmon trout, trout or salmon

1 egg yolk, beaten to blend

1 In a large pot, heat butter until it takes on a golden color. Add spinach, salt, pepper and nutmeg and cook over medium-high heat for 4 minutes. Drain in a colander. When spinach has cooled sufficiently to handle, squeeze out excess moisture.

2 Preheat oven to 450°F. Roll out half the puff pastry into a 25- x 2-inch rectangle ¼ inch thick. Cover pastry with spinach, leaving a narrow border around the edges. Place the smoked fish on top of the spinach.

3 Roll out a second strip of puff pastry slightly larger than the first. Brush the edges of the bottom strip of pastry with egg yolk. Cover the spinach and fish with the second pastry strip, pressing the edges together with your fingers. Brush the top with egg yolk. Bake for 12 minutes. Using a sharp knife, trim the edges, then cut crosswise into 4 portions. Serve hot.

Serve with cocktails, chilled Chablis or California champagne.

Salmon with Sage in a Pastry Case

Makes 4 servings

1 piece (4" x 6" x 1/4") puff pastry, commercial or homemade

1 tablespoon unsalted butter

1 tablespoon chopped shallot

1/2 cup dry white wine

1 cup heavy cream

salt and cayenne pepper

1 teaspoon unsalted butter

1 pound fresh salmon, sliced 1/16 inch thick in the style of smoked salmon

1/2 cup chopped fresh sage (or 2 tablespoons dried)

A salmon is born in a river, spends a good part of its adult life at sea, and returns to the river to spawn or to be caught. Because of pollution, overfishing and dam construction, this formerly common food is no longer as plentiful as it once was. Fortunately, however, several countries have started breeding farms in unpolluted waters. Salmon trout can also be used in this recipe. (Photo opposite page 147.)

1 Preheat oven to 400°F. Sprinkle a baking sheet with water and place the puff pastry on it. Prick the pastry well with a fork. Place a heatproof cup or tin, about 2 inches high, on each corner of the baking sheet; rest a wire rack on top of them (this will prevent the puff pastry from rising unevenly). Bake for 15 minutes. Reduce oven temperature to 350°F and bake until pastry is golden, about 12 minutes more. Cool on a rack. Cut the cooled pastry into 4 equal rectangles.

2 Melt 1 tablespoon butter in a small nonaluminum saucepan over medium-high heat. Add shallot and cook until soft and yellow but not brown. Add wine and boil until reduced to 2 tablespoons liquid. Add cream, salt and cayenne pepper and boil for 4 minutes, stirring constantly. Keep sauce warm.

3 Melt 1 teaspoon butter in a large skillet over high heat. Add salmon and cook for about 2 seconds on each side.

4 Split each rectangle of puff pastry open as though cutting a roll for a sandwich. Place the bottom halves on 4 separate plates. Divide about half of the salmon over the pastry; top with the upper half of the pastry and finish with another layer of salmon. Spoon sauce over and around the pastry. Sprinkle with chopped sage and serve.

Wine—Muscadet or California Chardonnay, served chilled.

Macaroni, Fennel and Sardine Pie

Makes 4 servings

1 pound fennel
1/3 cup golden raisins
2 pounds fresh large sardines
1 cup olive oil
5 shallots, chopped
3 salt-preserved or canned anchovies, chopped
pinch of saffron
1 pound elbow macaroni
2/3 cup pine nuts

The word "sardine" refers to young herring, pilchards and sprats. The name comes from the place where these small fish were first caught—the island of Sardinia. This dish originated in Corsica, my birthplace. (Photo 3 following page 146.)

1 Drop fennel into a large pot of boiling salted water and boil for 10 minutes. Remove with a slotted spoon; reserve cooking water.

2 Soak raisins in hot water for 15 minutes. Drain and set aside.

3 Remove and discard heads and backbones of sardines. Rinse fish and pat dry. Chop into 1-inch pieces.

4 Heat olive oil in a large skillet over high heat. Add shallots and cook, stirring, until lightly colored but not brown. Add sardines, fennel, anchovies and saffron and cook for 5 minutes, stirring occasionally. Remove from heat and set aside.

5 Preheat oven to 375°F.

6 Bring fennel cooking liquid to a boil. Drop in macaroni and cook until al dente. Drain, reserving 6 tablespoons cooking liquid.

7 Oil a 3-quart baking pan and spread half the macaroni over the bottom. Over it arrange the sardine mixture. Sprinkle with pine nuts and raisins and top with the remaining macaroni. Sprinkle with reserved macaroni cooking liquid. Bake for 15 minutes. Serve hot.

Wine—Chianti or California Zinfandel, served at room temperature.

Smoked Trout Pâté

Makes 4 servings

2 slices white bread
$1/4$ cup milk
$1/2$ pound lemon sole fillets
$1/2$ pound whiting fillets
salt and freshly ground white pepper
$1 1/4$ cups heavy cream
1 large smoked trout, filleted and cut into strips
10 sorrel leaves, chopped
2 tablespoons chopped watercress plus 12 whole leaves for garnish
1 envelope unflavored gelatin
1 cup water
2 tablespoons Cognac

A fish pâté is an elegant first course or light luncheon dish. The food processor makes it possible for the home cook to turn out pâté, which previously called for the laborious process of forcing the fish through a fine sieve. Smoked salmon can be used in place of smoked trout. *(Photo 3 following page 178.)*

1 Soak the bread in the milk for a few minutes. Combine the sole and whiting in a food processor fitted with the steel blade. Process for 25 seconds, stopping to scrape down the sides of the bowl. Add the bread and milk and process a few seconds longer. Season with salt and pepper to taste. With the machine running, slowly add the cream and blend until smooth.

2 Line a 1-quart terrine with plastic wrap. Spread half the fish mixture in the bottom of the terrine. Arrange the smoked trout strips on top, then add the remaining fish mixture. Sprinkle with chopped sorrel and watercress. Refrigerate for 1 hour.

3 Preheat oven to 300°F. Cover the terrine with foil and place in a larger baking pan. Add water to come halfway up the sides of the terrine. Bake for $1 1/2$ hours, or until a knife inserted into fish mixture comes out clean. (Or insert knife into fish mixture. Withdraw it and press it under your lower lip. If it feels hot, terrine is ready.) Remove terrine from water bath and cool to room temperature, then cover with aluminum foil and a weight. Refrigerate for at least 6 hours before serving.

4 After the terrine has been refrigerated for at least 6 hours, turn out on a platter. The bottom of the pâté will now be on top. Remove plastic wrap and decorate the top with the whole watercress leaves.

5 In a small saucepan sprinkle gelatin over 1 cup water. Let stand for 1 minute to soften, then stir over low heat until the gelatin is completely dissolved. Add the Cognac. Stir the gelatin over ice until it becomes syrupy, then coat the terrine with a layer of gelatin. Refrigerate until gelatin is set.

6 To prepare sauce: Mix yogurt and mayonnaise. Add the sorrel and watercress and season to taste. Serve with pâté.

Wine—Meursault or California Chardonnay, served chilled.

SORREL SAUCE

1 cup plain yogurt

1/2 cup homemade mayonnaise (see page 183)

2 1/2 tablespoons chopped sorrel

2 1/2 tablespoons chopped watercress

salt and freshly ground white pepper

Swordfish Pie Ajaccienne

This savory Corsican pie is named for the city of Ajaccio, Napoleon's birthplace. Tuna can also be used in this recipe. (Photo 3 following page 18.)

Makes 4 servings

CRUST

$1^1/_2$ cups plus 2 tablespoons all-purpose flour

$^1/_2$ cup sugar

grated zest of 1 lemon

pinch of salt

7 tablespoons cold unsalted butter, cut into small dice

3 egg yolks

2 tablespoons water

To prepare pastry:

1 Combine flour, sugar, lemon zest and salt. Add butter and rub with fingertips until mixture is the consistency of coarse meal.

2 Combine egg yolks and water. Add to flour mixture, blending rapidly with fingers to form a ball. Knead for 1 minute on a lightly floured surface. Cut dough in half.

3 Flatten each piece slightly into a disc. Wrap in plastic and refrigerate for at least 1 hour before using.

Meanwhile, prepare the filling:

1 Heat 4 tablespoons oil in a skillet over medium heat. Add onions and sauté, stirring occasionally, until evenly browned.

2 Combine tomato paste, celery, olives, capers and fish. Stir into onions and season with salt and pepper. Set aside.

3 Whisk egg and flour together. Dip zucchini into egg mixture and fry in the remaining 4 tablespoons oil over medium heat until lightly browned.

4 Preheat oven to 350°F. Roll out half of dough to fit an 8-inch pie pan 2½ inches deep. Spread fish mixture over dough and top with zucchini. Roll out remaining dough and cover filling. Crimp edges of dough and brush with beaten egg. Bake until crust is golden, about 50 minutes. Serve at room temperature.

Wine—Moulin à Vent or California Zinfandel, served cool.

FILLING

8 tablespoons olive oil

2 medium onions, chopped

2 tablespoons tomato paste

2 stalks celery, finely chopped

½ cup green olives, pitted and chopped

2 tablespoons capers

1 pound swordfish, cut into ¼-inch dice

salt and freshly ground white pepper

1 egg

2 teaspoons all-purpose flour

3 small zucchini, unpeeled, cut into 2-inch strips

1 egg, beaten

Pan Bagna

Makes 4 servings

4 French-style rolls or 1 baguette

2 cans ($6^{1}/_{2}$ to 7 ounces each) white-meat tuna

salt and freshly ground black pepper

1 tablespoon red wine vinegar

3 tablespoons virgin olive oil

1 head Bibb lettuce, separated into leaves, washed and dried

2 ripe tomatoes, sliced

1 large onion, sliced

1 can (2 ounces) anchovy fillets

20 Niçoise olives

There are many recipes for Pan Bagna, a specialty of the French Mediterranean coast; it is found in cafes and markets and is very often sold by street vendors. It is great picnic fare and should be made hours ahead, preferably the night before. In France, Pan Bagna is usually made with a round roll. In Le Vieux Nice, *the oldest part of the famous city on the French Riviera, Pan Bagna is part of the daily menu of the old brasseries that are lined up one after another along the narrow cobblestone streets. Since it is practically impossible to purchase a round French roll here, oval rolls or one long baguette will do. (Photo opposite.)*

1 Split the rolls or bread in half horizontally and place each bottom half on a sheet of aluminum foil. Cover the bottoms of the rolls or bread with the tuna.

2 In a mixing bowl, combine salt and pepper, vinegar and olive oil. Add lettuce, tomatoes and onion and coat with dressing. Pile on top of tuna. Add anchovy fillets and top with olives. Cover with the other half of the rolls or bread and wrap tightly with the aluminum foil. Turn upside down and let stand for several hours or overnight.

Serve with chilled beer, white wine or rosé.

Opposite: Pan Bagna (page 162).
Page following: Fish Soup with Saffron (page 170).

Stocks and Soups

Opposite: Monkfish Soup Catalane (page 172).
Page preceding: Summer Soup of Tuna and Salmon Trout (page 173).

Clam Chowder My Way

Makes 4 servings

2 tablespoons unsalted butter

3 dozen littleneck clams, shelled and chopped

3 large onions, chopped

3 large boiling potatoes, peeled and minced

1 bouquet garni, consisting of 1 bay leaf, 2 sprigs thyme, 1 stalk celery and 1/2 bunch flat-leaf parsley

pinch of nutmeg

pinch of cayenne pepper

2 cups Alsatian Riesling

1 cup fish fumet (see page 169)

1/2 cup cracker crumbs

salt and freshly ground white pepper

This is a French chef's version of clam chowder. Accompany with oyster crackers.

1 Melt butter in a large kettle or stockpot over low heat. Add clams and onions, cover tightly and cook 3 minutes. Add potatoes and bouquet garni and cook 5 minutes. Stir with a wooden spoon and add nutmeg, cayenne, wine and fish fumet. Simmer uncovered for 25 minutes.

2 Remove bouquet garni and stir cracker crumbs into chowder. Season to taste with salt and pepper. Serve hot.

Wine—Alsatian Riesling or California Chardonnay, served chilled.

Codfish Soup New Delhi

The Indian influence gives unique flavor to an old standby—fish soup. Pollack can also be used in this recipe.

Makes 4 servings

1 codfish (3 pounds), cleaned
1 pound eel or 1 snapper head
4 cups water
2 cups Muscadet
1 bouquet garni, consisting of 1 bay leaf, 2 sprigs thyme, 1 stalk celery and 1/2 bunch flat-leaf parsley
2 tablespoons unsalted butter
1 large onion, minced
1 leek, white and light green parts only, cleaned and minced
2 tablespoons all-purpose flour
2 tablespoons curry powder
4 egg yolks
3 tablespoons heavy cream
salt and freshly ground white pepper

1 Cut cod into fillets, reserving bones and head. Place fillets in a large saucepan or Dutch oven. Chop eel or fish heads and bones and add to fish. Add water, wine and bouquet garni and cook at a lively simmer for 25 minutes.

2 Remove fish and cut into 1-inch dice. Strain stock. Discard eel and heads.

3 Melt butter in a large saucepan. Add onion and leek and sauté over medium-high heat until golden. Stir in flour and curry powder. Add fish and cook for 3 minutes.

4 Transfer fish to a tureen. Add reserved stock to the saucepan and simmer for 15 minutes.

5 Combine egg yolks and cream. Whisk into the stock and cook gently until lightly thickened; do not boil. Season with salt and pepper. Pour over fish and serve.

Wine—Muscadet or California Dry Riesling, served chilled.

Court Bouillon with Milk

Makes enough to poach a 2- to 3-pound fish

1 cup milk
2 cups water
2 sprigs fresh thyme (or $^1/_4$ teaspoon dried)
2 bay leaves
5 whole black peppercorns
1 stalk celery
2 whole cloves
salt or sea salt

Since emphasis is currently being placed on the importance of eating fish rich in fats of the Omega-3 family, this court bouillon is designed for poaching just such fish. Salmon, mackerel, tuna and bluefish are some of the most popular examples.

Combine all ingredients in a fish poacher or a pot large enough to hold the fish. Bring to a boil; reduce heat and simmer uncovered for 15 minutes. Cool and use as required.

Court Bouillon with White Wine

Court bouillon lends flavor to poached fish and can be refrigerated for several days or frozen for several months.

Makes about 2½ cups

1 cup dry white wine
2 cups water
1 small carrot, peeled and sliced
1 leek, white and light green parts only, cleaned and sliced
1 stalk celery
1 white onion, sliced
1 sprig fresh thyme (or ⅛ teaspoon dried)
2 bay leaves
5 whole white peppercorns

Combine all ingredients in a large nonaluminum saucepan and bring to boil. Allow to boil for 20 minutes. Strain through a fine sieve, pressing down on the solids to extract as much flavor as possible.

Diet Court Bouillon

Makes enough for poaching a 2- to 3-pound whole fish

1 cup dry white wine
1/2 cup white wine vinegar
2 cups water
1 small carrot, peeled and sliced
1 leek, cleaned and sliced
1 stalk celery, sliced
1 white onion, sliced
1 sprig fresh thyme (or 1/4 teaspoon dried)
2 bay leaves
2 sprigs fresh tarragon (or 1/4 teaspoon dried)
5 peppercorns
sea salt

This is called diet court bouillon because the wine and vinegar help to remove the fish fat. It is particularly well suited for poaching bass or pike.

Combine all ingredients in a large nonaluminum saucepan and bring to boil. Continue to boil for 20 minutes. Strain through a fine strainer, pressing down on the solids to extract as much flavor as possible. Use as needed.

Fish Fumet

Fish fumet, or broth, is the base for a multitude of soups and sauces. It can be prepared ahead and refrigerated for several days or frozen for a longer period.

Since it is a base for other recipes, we haven't added salt. The amount will depend on the mixture in which the broth is used.

Makes 2 quarts

2 tablespoons unsalted butter

3 pounds fish bones (sole, halibut, turbot, eel and/or bass)

2 carrots, diced

2 onions, diced

2 stalks celery, diced

3 cloves garlic

2 sprigs fresh thyme (or 1/4 teaspoon dried)

2 bay leaves

4 parsley sprigs

8 white peppercorns

4 cups dry white wine

6 cups water

1 Melt butter in a large non-aluminum saucepan over high heat. Add fish bones, reduce heat to low, cover and cook for 5 minutes. Add all the vegetables, herbs and peppercorns and stir for 3 minutes over high heat. Add the wine and water and simmer for 20 minutes, skimming the accumulated scum that forms at the top for the first few minutes.

2 Strain the broth into another saucepan, pressing down to extract as much liquid as possible from the solids. Boil until reduced to 2 quarts. Cool the broth immediately over a bowl of ice cubes and refrigerate or freeze.

Fish Soup with Saffron

Makes 4 servings

1 pound fish bones (preferably sole or eel)
1 onion, sliced
1 bunch parsley
2 quarts cold water
3 tablespoons olive oil
1 carrot, chopped
1 leek, chopped
1 tomato, peeled, seeded and chopped
1 bouquet garni, consisting of 1 bay leaf, 2 sprigs of fresh thyme (or 1/4 teaspoon dried), 1 stalk celery and 1/2 bunch flat-leaf parsley
1 clove garlic, chopped
pinch of saffron
2 tablespoons heavy cream
salt and freshly ground black pepper
3/4 pound fish fillets (monkfish, whiting and unskinned red snapper), cut into small pieces
fresh chervil leaves

Redolent of olive oil and saffron, and with a minimal amount of cream, this soup makes a fine one-course luncheon served with plenty of crusty French bread. (Photo 2 following page 162.)

1 Combine fish bones, onion, parsley and water in a large saucepan and bring to boil. Let boil for 15 minutes. Strain the broth through a very fine strainer or cheesecloth into another saucepan.

2 Heat olive oil in a Dutch oven over high heat. Add carrot and leek and sauté for about 10 minutes, stirring. Add tomato and cook for 5 minutes. Add bouquet garni and garlic to fish stock and bring to boil. Add saffron and simmer for 40 minutes.

3 Preheat oven to 375°F. Heat 4 soup bowls in oven until very hot. Stir cream into soup and season with salt and pepper. Pour 1 cup soup into each bowl and divide fish equally among the bowls. Bake for 2 minutes. Sprinkle with chervil and serve.

Wine—Côte de Bellet, Rosé d'Anjou or California Dry Rosé, served chilled.

Leek, Watercress and Cod Soup

The fish is quickly cooked by the boiling pale green soup as it is poured into the bowl. Any white-fleshed fish is suitable—hake, whiting or bass, for example.

Makes 4 servings

2 tablespoons butter
1 large onion, sliced
2 leeks, white and pale green parts only, cleaned and minced
2 cups fish fumet (see page 169)
1 cup heavy cream
2 bunches watercress, heavy stems removed (reserve 20 large leaves for garnish)
salt and freshly ground white pepper
1 pound cod, hake, whiting or bass fillets, cut into 1/2-inch squares
2 tablespoons whipped cream
1 teaspoon paprika

1 In a heavy pot, heat the butter until light brown. Add onion and leeks and cover with a round of waxed paper cut to the exact diameter of the pan. Cover the pot with a lid and cook over low heat for 3 minutes. Add the fish fumet and cream and cook uncovered over medium heat for 15 minutes. Add the 2 bunches of watercress and boil for exactly 4 minutes. Puree in a food processor or food mill. Add salt and pepper to taste. Return to pot and boil again for 2 minutes.

2 Divide the raw fish among 4 soup bowls. Pour on the boiling soup and garnish with the watercress leaves. Top with a half tablespoon of whipped cream and sprinkle with paprika. Serve immediately.

Wine—Chablis or California Chardonnay, served chilled.

Monkfish Soup Catalane

Makes 4 servings

2 pounds monkfish, cut into large chunks

2 quarts fish fumet (see page 169)

5 slices smoked ham, cut into 1/2-inch squares

6 large shrimp

1 cup fresh or frozen peas

1 sweet red pepper, seeded and cut into 1/2-inch squares

6 tablespoons homemade mayonnaise, prepared with lemon (see page 183)

salt and freshly ground white pepper

homemade croutons

From Catalonia, on the shores of the Mediterranean, this typically Spanish assemblage makes a richly satisfying one-dish meal. Swordfish can also be used in this recipe. (Photo opposite page 163.)

1 Combine the fish, fish broth, ham, shrimp, peas and red pepper in a 4-quart pot. Bring to simmer; continue to simmer for 25 minutes.

2 Transfer 3 cups broth to another saucepan and maintain at a simmer. Whisk in mayonnaise; continue whisking until liquid becomes pale.

3 Stir mixture back into the larger pot. Season to taste with salt and pepper.

4 Serve in soup bowls and top with croutons.

Wine—Blanc de Blancs or California Chenin Blanc, served chilled.

Summer Soup of Tuna and Salmon Trout

At last tuna has come into its own in this country as a fresh fish—no longer conjuring up visions of canned tuna salad. Not quite as easy to find, salmon trout, a pink-fleshed member of the trout family, can be found at a good fishmonger's and is worth looking for.

This refreshing warm-weather soup lies somewhere between a gazpacho and a ceviche. Sea bass or salmon can also be used in this recipe. (Photo 3 following page 162.)

Makes 4 servings

2 pounds tomatoes
1 sweet red pepper
1 cucumber
1 clove garlic
salt
2 tablespoons sherry vinegar
1/4 cup virgin olive oil
2 drops Tabasco sauce
1 white onion
2 tablespoons chopped fresh mint
1/2 pound tuna fillets
1/2 pound salmon trout
juice of 1 lemon

1 Plunge the tomatoes into boiling water for 1 minute. Cool in ice water and remove the skins. Cut the tomatoes in half crosswise and squeeze out the seeds and juice.

2 Cut the pepper in half and remove the seeds. Peel the cucumber, cut it in half lengthwise and remove the seeds. Combine tomato, 1/2 pepper, 1/2 cucumber and garlic in a blender or food processor and puree. Stir in salt, vinegar, olive oil and Tabasco sauce.

3 Cut the onion and the remaining 1/2 cucumber and 1/2 pepper into small dice. Combine the diced vegetables and the mint in a bowl and refrigerate for 10 minutes.

4 To serve: Cut the tuna and trout into julienne strips. Add the lemon juice and salt to taste. Place the fish in chilled bowls and pour the vegetable puree over. Sprinkle each bowl with diced vegetables and mint.

Serve with chilled spring water, Entre-Deux-Mers or a New York State white wine.

Clam and Corn Chowder

Makes 4 servings

1 large onion, sliced
2 tablespoons unsalted butter
1 can (17 ounces) whole kernel corn, undrained
2 dozen littleneck clams
1 cup heavy cream
4 slices crisply cooked bacon, chopped
salt and freshly ground black pepper
1 tablespoon chopped fresh parsley

1 In a large skillet, sauté onion in butter until golden. Add corn and liquid and cook for 6 minutes.

2 Open clams, reserving their liquor. Keep the meat in the refrigerator.

3 Bring clam liquor to a boil with cream. Puree onion, corn and cream mixture in a food processor and return to boil.

4 Divide raw clam meat and bacon among small soup bowls. Add cream mixture and salt and pepper to taste; top with parsley. Serve hot.

Wine—California Fumé Blanc or Meursault, served chilled.

Sauces

Sauce Américaine or Armoricaine

Makes 2 quarts

3 tablespoons virgin olive oil

3 lobsters, 1 pound each (or 3 pounds crabs or crayfish)

2 onions, chopped

2 small carrots, peeled and cut into 1/2-inch dice

2 stalks celery, cut into 1/2-inch dice

4 cloves garlic, minced

1 bouquet garni consisting of parsley, thyme and tarragon

2 bay leaves

1/2 cup Cognac or other brandy

2 cups dry white wine

3 ripe tomatoes, quartered

3 tablespoons tomato paste

2 tablespoons beef stock base or 1 beef bouillon cube

2 quarts fish fumet (page 169)

pinch of cayenne pepper

There are a number of theories as to the origin of this sauce, one being that it originated in Brittany as Sauce Armoricaine and that somehow the spelling changed to Américaine. Whatever its origin, it is marvelous with lobster, crabs and other seafood, or as a base for soups.

The lobster meat used in the recipe can be removed from the shell and eaten with the sauce, or made into a salad.

1 Heat the olive oil in a large stockpot until very hot. Add the lobsters and stir until the shells turn red. Add all the diced vegetables, garlic, bouquet garni and bay leaves. Cover the contents of the pot by placing a round of waxed paper, cut to the diameter of the pot, directly on top. Turn the heat to low, cover with the pot lid, and cook for 7 minutes, or until the vegetables are slightly browned. Discard waxed paper.

2 Add Cognac and wine and boil for 3 minutes. (It is not necessary to flambé the alcohol, as the boiling will evaporate it.) Add the tomatoes, tomato paste, beef base, fish fumet and cayenne pepper, and boil for 35 minutes. Strain and boil again for 5 minutes.

Anchovy Sauce

This sauce for salads or hard-cooked eggs can be kept several weeks in the refrigerator.

Makes about 2¾ cups

2 cans (2 ounces each) anchovies in olive oil, drained

2 cloves garlic

2 sprigs fresh thyme (or ¼ teaspoon dried)

1½ tablespoons Dijon-style mustard

3 tablespoons red wine vinegar

freshly ground black pepper

2 cups virgin olive oil

Combine all ingredients except oil in a blender or food processor and puree for about 1 minute. With the machine running, add the oil in a thin stream and process until the mixture is thick and smooth.

Bechamel Sauce

Makes about 2 cups

$1\frac{1}{2}$ cups milk

2 tablespoons unsalted butter

2 tablespoons all-purpose flour

salt and freshly ground white pepper

$\frac{1}{8}$ teaspoon nutmeg

In France, bechamel is known as a "mother sauce"; it is not served as is. Combined with egg yolks and beaten egg whites, it serves as a soufflé base; with the addition of cheese it is Mornay sauce; and flavored with crustacean shells, it becomes Sauce Nantua.

1 Heat milk to simmering point. Meanwhile, melt butter in a heavy-bottomed saucepan. Add flour and stir with a wooden spoon over medium heat until mixture is yellow and foamy but not browned, about 2 minutes.

2 Remove from heat and quickly whisk in milk. Return to medium heat and cook, stirring constantly, until mixture thickens, about 5 minutes. Season with salt, pepper and nutmeg.

Opposite: Ravioli of Scallops (page 138).
Page following: Shrimp Riviera (page 143).

White Butter Sauce (Beurre Blanc)

The Nantais (natives of Nantes, a town in Brittany) boast that they make the best beurre blanc *in the world, and they are probably right.*

A Brochet de la Loire, *or pike,* au Beurre Blanc, *savored on a shady terrace along the banks of the Erdre and washed down with a chilled Muscadet, makes an unforgettable meal.*

Makes 4 servings

3 tablespoons white wine vinegar

$^1/_2$ cup dry white wine

2 tablespoons chopped shallot

1 teaspoon crushed white pepper

$1^1/_2$ tablespoons crème fraîche or heavy cream

12 tablespoons ($1^1/_2$ sticks) unsalted butter, cut into small pieces

salt

In a nonaluminum medium saucepan, combine the vinegar, wine, shallot and white pepper and boil over high heat until reduced to 2 tablespoons. Add the cream and boil 2 minutes. Remove from heat and whisk in the butter one piece at a time. Strain the sauce, season with salt, and serve immediately.

Note: This sauce is very fragile. It's best to make it at the last minute.

Opposite: Shellfish Omelet Côte Opale (page 132).
Page preceding: Smoked Trout Pâté (page 158).

Sauce Grelette for Cold Fish

Makes 4 servings

1 cup heavy cream
3 tomatoes, peeled, seeded and diced
2 tablespoons Cognac or other brandy
1/4 cup ketchup
1 tablespoon finely chopped fresh parsley
1 tablespoon finely chopped fresh tarragon
1 tablespoon finely chopped fresh chervil
salt and freshly ground white pepper

It may be surprising coming from a French chef, but ketchup is one of the components of this sauce. We don't know the origin of the name but the sauce is delicious. It also contains wonderful herbs—parsley, tarragon and chervil.

Whip cream in a mixing bowl to soft peaks. Fold in diced tomatoes. Add Cognac and ketchup, mixing gently. Then add the herbs and season to taste with salt and pepper.

Hollandaise Sauce

This most important emulsified sauce, which serves as a base for innumerable other sauces, is worth mastering. With the addition of orange rind it becomes sauce Maltaise; with mint, Paloise; with meat glaze, Smitaine and so on. Tarragon, dill, thyme, chives, sorrel, basil—any one can be added. The flavor can be varied by the use of Pernod, vodka or vermouth. Purees of tomato, watercress, horseradish or avocado also add delicious flavor and attractive color.

In preparing hollandaise, it's most important that the water in the lower part of the double boiler not boil or touch the upper pot. If this rule is not observed, the result will be scrambled eggs rather than a smooth sauce.

Makes 4 servings

3 large egg yolks
2 tablespoons water or dry white wine
*1/2 cup clarified butter**
juice of 1/2 lemon
salt and freshly ground white pepper

In the lower part of a double boiler, heat water to the simmering point. Combine the egg yolks and water or wine in the top of the double boiler and place over the lower half. Whisk rapidly for 4 minutes, making sure that the water underneath never boils. When the egg mixture is very fluffy and light, whisk in the clarified butter a tablespoon at a time, cooking until the sauce has thickened. Add lemon juice, salt and pepper. Serve hot.

**Clarified butter is butter that is heated and melted. The clear yellow liquid that remains on top is the clarified butter. It is used in making sauces and for sautéing because it does not burn as easily as butter that is not clarified.*

To clarify butter, cut it into 1-inch slices and place in a saucepan over medium heat. After the butter melts, skim off foam from top, strain yellow liquid into a bowl and discard the milky residue remaining at the bottom of the saucepan.

Horseradish Sauce

Makes 4 servings

1/3 cup heavy cream

3 tablespoons grated fresh horseradish

1/3 teaspoon Dijon-style mustard

1 tablespoon white wine vinegar

pinch of sugar

A Danish sauce, this is usually served with cold fish, roast beef or sandwiches of cold cuts.

Whip cream to soft peaks in mixing bowl. Whisk in remaining ingredients. Correct seasoning by adding more vinegar or sugar as necessary.

Mayonnaise

A classic cold sauce on its own, mayonnaise also forms the basis of many other sauces with the addition of a few ingredients. It can become gribiche *by adding hard-cooked egg yolks and mustard,* rémoulade *with gherkins, capers and herbs,* aïoli *with the addition of garlic and so on.*

It is essential that all ingredients be at room temperature; remove them from the refrigerator an hour ahead of time.

Makes 4 servings

2 large egg yolks
2 teaspoons Dijon-style mustard
2/3 cup peanut oil
4 teaspoons fresh lemon juice or 2 teaspoons red wine vinegar
salt and freshly ground white pepper

By hand:

In a mixing bowl, whisk together egg yolks and mustard. Whisk in 1/2 cup oil about 1 teaspoon at a time until sauce has thickened; then whisk in remaining oil a little more quickly. Add lemon juice or vinegar and salt and pepper to taste.

In a blender or food processor:

1 Combine egg yolks, mustard, lemon juice or vinegar, salt and pepper and process for about 15 seconds or until eggs become fluffy.

2 With machine running, pour oil through feed tube about a teaspoon at a time until mixture begins to thicken; then continue pouring a little more quickly until all the oil is incorporated. Adjust seasoning to taste.

Garlic Mayonnaise (Aïoli)

Makes 4 servings

12 cloves garlic, peeled and pureed
2 large egg yolks
1 teaspoon Dijon-style mustard
1 cup virgin olive oil
salt and freshly ground white pepper

Aïoli, usually eaten with poached white-fleshed fish or other seafood, is commonly served on Fridays in the south of France.

By hand:

In a mixing bowl, whisk pureed garlic with egg yolks and mustard. Whisk in 1/2 cup olive oil about 1 teaspoon at a time, then whisk in remaining oil a little more quickly; whisk until mixture is mayonnaise consistency. Season to taste with salt and pepper.

In a blender or food processor:

1 With machine running, drop garlic cloves through the feed tube and process until minced. Add the egg yolks, mustard, salt and pepper, processing until eggs become fluffy.

2 With machine running, pour the oil through the feed tube very slowly. When the mixture starts thickening, add the oil a little more quickly and continue processing until all is incorporated.

Mustard Sauce

This goes well with fish prepared in a variety of ways—grilled, poached or broiled.

Makes 4 servings

3 tablespoons unsalted butter
1 tablespoon all-purpose flour
2 tablespoons milk
2 tablespoons Dijon-style mustard
salt

1 Melt the butter in a small saucepan over low heat. Whisk in the flour, then the milk and cook for 6 minutes, stirring constantly. Whisk in the mustard, being careful not to allow the sauce to boil and foam. Remove from heat and season to taste with salt.

2 If by accident the sauce does boil, causing it to separate, it can be emulsified by beating it in a food processor or by shaking it vigorously in a covered jar.

Cold Saffron Sauce

Makes 4 servings

1 baked potato or 1/4 cup dried potato flakes combined with 1/4 cup water

2 large egg yolks

1 cup olive oil

few strands of Spanish saffron combined with 2 tablespoons hot water

salt and freshly ground white pepper

Known as rouille, *this is a type of mayonnaise from the south of France. It is used on white-fleshed fish, in soups and for barbecued foods.*

By hand:

Remove pulp from baked potato and puree. Place the potato puree in a large bowl and whisk in the egg yolks. Whisk in the olive oil, 1 teaspoon at a time at first, then a little more rapidly as the sauce emulsifies. Add the dissolved saffron and water. Season with salt and pepper.

In a blender or food processor:

1 Combine potato pulp, egg yolks, dissolved saffron and water, salt and pepper in a blender or processor. Blend for about 15 seconds until well combined.

2 With machine running, pour the oil through the feed tube very slowly. When the mixture starts thickening, add the oil a little more quickly and continue processing until it is all incorporated.

Cold Sorrel Sauce

It is important that the sorrel be cut into the thinnest possible julienne and that it be added at the last minute—just before serving. Always use stainless steel or glass bowls to prevent discoloration.

Makes 4 servings

- *1/3 cup heavy cream*
- *3 tablespoons mayonnaise, preferably homemade (see page 183)*
- *1 teaspoon chopped fresh parsley*
- *1 teaspoon chopped fresh chervil*
- *2 tablespoons sorrel, cut into very thin julienne*
- *salt and freshly ground white pepper*

In a mixing bowl, whip the heavy cream to soft peaks. Gently stir in remaining ingredients.

Sweden Sauce

Makes 4 servings

1/4 cup mustard, preferably Grey Poupon, which is milder than other Dijon-style mustards

2 tablespoons dark brown sugar

2 large egg yolks

1/2 cup peanut oil

salt and freshly ground white pepper

3 tablespoons finely chopped fresh dill

Sweden sauce is most often served with gravlax; it's delicious on its own or combined with hollandaise, white butter sauce or mayonnaise. The uses of this versatile sauce are limited only by your imagination.

By hand:

In a mixing bowl, whisk mustard, brown sugar and egg yolks to combine, then whisk in the peanut oil about 1 teaspoon at a time. Continue to whisk until the consistency of mayonnaise. Whisk in salt, pepper and dill.

In a blender or food processor:

1 Combine mustard, brown sugar, egg yolks, salt and pepper in a blender or processor. Blend for about 15 seconds.

2 With processor running, pour the oil through the feed tube very slowly. When the mixture starts thickening, add the oil a little more quickly and continue processing until it is all incorporated. Stir in dill.

Fast Tomato Sauce

This versatile sauce can be served over rice, pasta, grilled or poached fish, or even cauliflower.

Makes 4 servings

2 tablespoons virgin olive oil
1 small white onion, chopped
1 stalk celery
1 small carrot, peeled and sliced
2 cloves garlic, minced
1 sprig fresh thyme (or 1/4 teaspoon dried)
1 bay leaf
5 ripe tomatoes, sliced
1 teaspoon chicken stock base or 1/4 chicken bouillon cube
salt and freshly ground black pepper

Heat olive oil in a saucepan over high heat. Add onion, celery, carrot, garlic, thyme and bay leaf and sauté for 7 minutes. Add the remaining ingredients and cook for 10 minutes. Discard bay leaf. Transfer sauce to a food processor or blender and puree. Strain and reheat in a small saucepan.

Vinaigrette

A basic vinaigrette dressing mellowed with a bit of crème fraîche.

Makes about 1 cup

1/3 cup wine vinegar
1/2 cup peanut oil
1 1/2 tablespoons crème fraîche
salt and freshly ground black pepper

Place vinegar in a nonaluminum bowl and whisk in the peanut oil, then the crème fraîche. Season to taste with salt and pepper.

Wine and Food Guide

Imported Wine and Food Guide

Wine	Dishes
Aligoté	*Kippers Mermaid* Page 26 *Steamed Porgy with Seaweed* Page 40 *Grilled Grouper with Creamed Leeks* Page 69 *Grouper Fillet Madras* Page 70 *Cold Skate and Tomato* Page 92 *Witches' Pot* Page 117
Alsatian Pinot Noir	*Sea Bass with Honey Vinegar and Artichoke Bottoms* Page 46
Alsatian Riesling	*Porgy with Bacon* Page 38 *Fillet of Lemon Sole with Leek and Sorrel* Page 100 *Smoked Trout Crystal* Page 106 *Crab with Fennel* Page 113 *Prawns Early Morning* Page 142 *Quiche of Crabmeat and Endive* Page 151 *Clam Chowder My Way* Page 164
Alsatian Sylvaner	*Pike with Mushroom Scales* Page 35 *Squid Colin Maillard* Page 145 *Sea Urchins in a Spinach Nest* Page 148
Beaujolais	*Grilled Eel with Tartar Sauce* Page 23 *Codfish Père Claude* Page 65 *Bay Scallops with Pasta and Wild Mushrooms* Page 137

Chablis	*Monkfish Cake with Tomatoes Page 79* *Red Snapper Baked Alaska Page 95* *Medallions of Turbot with Apple Page 110* *Madison Avenue Stuffed Clams Page 112* *Lobster Big Apple Page 123* *Leek, Watercress and Cod Soup Page 171*
Champagne	*Halibut Jacqueline in Champagne Sauce Page 75* *Pike Poached in Champagne Page 80*
Chardonnay from the Jura	*Stuffed Fresh Trout in Jail Page 57*
Châteauneuf du Pape (white)	*Ravioli of Scallops Page 138*
Chianti	*Herring with Love Apples Page 77* *Macaroni, Fennel and Sardine Pie Page 156*
Chianti Classico	*Pizza alla Porto Vecchio Page 152*
Côtes du Rhône Cairanne (white)	*Eels in a Dance of Herbs Page 24*
Coteaux du Layon	*Shrimp with Chives and Cinnamon Sauce Page 141*

Entre-Deux-Mers	*Lemon Sole with Gin Boulogne Page 103* *Summer Soup of Tuna with Salmon Trout Page 173*
Italian red (light)	*Eight Arms with Rice Page 130*
Juliénas	*Cold American Char Forestière Page 55* *Codfish with Shallots and Red Wine Page 66* *Flounder with Tomatoes and Sweet Garlic Sauce Page 68*
Mâcon	*Pike Soufflé with Crayfish Sauce Page 81*
Mâcon Viré	*Lemon Sole with Rice and Hard-Cooked Eggs Page 101* *Ceviche of Fish Page 94* *Baked Grey Sole with Swiss Cheese Page 97* *Grilled Tuna Maquis Page 109*
Mercurey (white)	*Perch in Chardonnay Page 34*
Mercurey (red)	*Grouper with Three Vegetables Page 71*
Meursault	*Baked Carp with Herb Stuffing Page 22*

Meursault	*Grey Sole Baked with Pearl Onions and Turnips Page 50* *Salmon Marinated with Oil and Herbs Page 86* *Minced Salmon Wilfried Page 90* *Sole, Spinach and Salmon Westbury Page 99* *Terrine of Black Bass and Asparagus Page 150* *Smoked Trout Pâté Page 158* *Clam and Corn Chowder Page 174*
Morgon	*Grilled Whiting and Savoy Cabbage Page 58*
Moulin à Vent	*Sautéed Haddock Mme. Colette Page 72* *Swordfish Pie Ajaccienne Page 160*
Muscadet	*Bluefish Ile de France Page 20* *Carp with Ale Page 21* *Mackerel Marinated in Muscadet Page 30* *Baked Whole Grey Sole with Fresh Herbs Page 53* *Fried Sardines France Page 43* *Porgy with Sea Urchin Sauce Page 41* *Baked Red Snapper with Roasted Peanuts Page 49* *Grilled Yellow Pike in Shallot Sauce Page 37*

Muscadet	*Roast Monkfish with Sorrel* Page 78 *Wild Salmon Paillard Karine* Page 88 *Fresh Sturgeon Grand'mère* Page 104 *Tuna Poached in Cream* Page 108 *Poached Yellow Pike with Chives* Page 82 *Soft-Shell Crabs Sautéed with Hazelnuts or Pecans* Page 116 *Lobster Salad in Harlequin Dress* Page 126 *Salmon with Sage in a Pastry Case* Page 154 *Codfish Soup New Delhi* Page 165
Muscadet-sur-lie	*Mackerel on the Quay* Page 29 *Haricots Verts Salad with Langoustine and Hazelnut* Page 122 *Mussels Danielle* Page 127
Muscat from Languedoc	*Seafood Stew with Muscat Wine* Page 120
Portuguese Rosé	*Haddock and Potato Gratin* Page 73
Pouilly Fuissé	*Porgy Dauphinoise* Page 39 *Red Snapper with Fennel and Dill* Page 96 *Crab Caribbean* Page 114

Pouilly Fumé	*Warm Lobster Salad in Vermouth Butter Page 125*
	Mussels Sailor Fashion (Moules Marinière) Page 128
Provençale white	*Soft-Shell Crab in Two Blankets Page 115*
Rosé Côtes de Bellet	*Baked Flounder with Orange Page 24*
	Poached Pollack Onzainoise Page 83
	Skate with Spinach and Pink Grapefruit Salad Page 93
	Fish Soup with Saffron Page 170
Rosé de Provence	*Mullet Saint-Tropez Page 33*
	Sardines with Mint Napoleon Page 44
	Roasted Red Snapper with Bay Leaves and Citrus Page 45
	Striped Bass with Bacon Mediterranean Style Page 60
	Fresh Codfish Daudet Page 63
	Poached Codfish Fillets Chistera Page 64
	Raw Halibut with Pernod Page 74
	John Dory, My Way Page 28
	Grilled Swordfish with Horseradish Sauce Page 105
	Crayfish Salad with Citrus Vinaigrette Page 118
	Shrimp Riviera Page 143

Rosé Lirac	*Red Mullet with Orange and Leeks Page 32*
Saint-Tropez white	*Joel's Barbecued Maine Lobster Page 124*
Sancerre	*Skate with Almonds Page 91* *Shellfish Omelet Côte Opale Page 132* *Shrimp with Sour Cream Blésoise Page 144*
Sauternes	*Belon Oysters in Sauce Sauternes Page 131*
Sparkling Vouvray	*Shad Braised with Sorrel Page 48* *Halibut Jacqueline in Champagne Sauce Page 75* *Blue Point Oysters and Clams with Green Herbs Page 135*
Tavel Rosé	*Pompano Fillets with Scallion Page 84* *Kabob of Sea Scallops with Garlic Butter Page 136* *Squid with Ham Bernadette Page 147*

Domestic Wine and Food Guide

Cabernet Rosé (California)	*Oysters Florida Fashion* Page 134 *Squid with Ham Bernadette* Page 147
Cabernet Sauvignon (California)	*Sea Bass with Honey Vinegar and Artichoke Bottoms* Page 46 *Grey Sole Paysanne* Page 52 *Codfish Père Claude* Page 65 *Bay Scallops with Pasta and Wild Mushrooms* Page 137 *Pizza alla Porto Vecchio* Page 152
Champagne (California)	*Shad Braised with Sorrel* Page 48 *Halibut Jacqueline in Champagne Sauce* Page 75 *Pike Poached in Champagne* Page 80
Chablis (California)	*Mussels Danielle* Page 127
Chardonnay (California)	*Baked Carp with Herb Stuffing* Page 22 *Perch in Chardonnay* Page 34 *Porgy with Bacon* Page 38 *Porgy Dauphinoise* Page 39 *Steamed Porgy with Seaweed* Page 40 *Stew of Brill with Vermouth and Tarragon* Page 62 *Roast Monkfish with Sorrel* Page 78 *Pike Soufflé with Crayfish Sauce* Page 81

Chardonnay (California)	*Salmon Marinated with Olive Oil and Herbs Page 86* *Skate with Almonds Page 91* *Sole, Spinach and Salmon Westbury Page 99* *Grilled Tuna Maquis Page 109* *Warm Lobster Salad in Vermouth Butter Page 125* *Salmon with Sage in a Pastry Case Page 154* *Smoked Trout Pâté Page 158* *Clam Chowder My Way Page 164* *Leek, Watercress and Cod Soup Page 171*
Chenin Blanc (California)	*Mackerel on the Quay Page 29* *Mullet Saint-Tropez Page 33* *Grey Sole Baked with Pearl Onions and Turnips Page 50* *Stuffed Fresh Trout in Jail Page 57* *Monkfish Cake with Tomatoes Page 78* *Lemon Sole with Rice and Hard-Cooked Eggs Page 101* *Minced Salmon Wilfried Page 90* *Cold Skate and Tomato Page 92* *Baked Grey Sole with Swiss Cheese Page 97*

Wine	Dishes
Chenin Blanc (California)	*Sautéed Lemon Sole with Tapenade* Page 102 *Fresh Sturgeon Grand'mère* Page 104 *Smoked Trout, Crystal* Page 106 *Tuna Poached in Cream* Page 108 *Medallions of Turbot with Apple* Page 110 *Poached Yellow Pike with Chives* Page 82 *Crab Caribbean* Page 114 *Crab with Fennel* Page 113 *Monkfish Soup Catalane* Page 172
French Colombard (California)	*Eels in a Dance of Herbs* Page 23 *Kippers Mermaid* Page 26 *Brill Corrick* Page 61 *Grilled Swordfish with Horseradish Sauce* Page 105 *Lobster Salad in Harlequin Dress* Page 126 *Quiche of Crabmeat and Endive* Page 151
Fumé Blanc (California)	*Baked Whole Grey Sole with Fresh Herbs* Page 53 *Haddock and Potato Gratin* Page 73 *Corn and Clam Chowder* Page 174
Gamay Beaujolais (California)	*Grilled Eel with Tartar Sauce* Page 23

Johannisberg Riesling (California)	*Shrimp with Chive and Cinnamon Sauce Page 141*
Mendocino County French Colombard	*Lemon Sole with Gin Boulogne Page 103*
Merlot (California)	*Eight Arms with Rice Page 130*
Napa Valley Sauvignon Blanc (California)	*Ceviche of Fish Page 94*
New York State white	*Soft-Shelled Crab Sautéed with Hazelnuts or Pecans Page 116* *Summer Soup of Tuna and Salmon Trout Page 173*
Pinot Noir (California)	*Barbecued Mackerel with Roquefort Sauce Page 31*
Pinot (California)	*Mussels and Squash in Cream Sauce Page 129* *Prawns Early Morning Page 142*
Riesling, Dry (California)	*Mackerel Marinated in Muscadet Page 30* *Grilled Yellow Pike in Shallot Sauce Page 37* *Fillet of Lemon Sole with Leek and Sorrel Page 100*

Riesling, Dry (California)	*Haricots Verts Salad with Langoustine and Hazelnuts* Page 122 *Codfish Soup New Delhi* Page 165
Rosé, Dry (California)	*Sole with Beets and Capers* Page 51 *Roasted Red Snapper with Bay Leaves and Citrus* Page 45 *Fish Soup with Saffron* Page 170
Sauvignon Blanc (California)	*Bluefish Ile de France* Page 20 *Pike with Mushroom Scales* Page 35 *Sole with Beets and Capers* Page 51 *Fried Sardines France* Page 43 *Porgy with Sea Urchin Sauce* Page 41 *Grilled Grouper with Creamed Leeks* Page 69 *Grouper Fillet Madras* Page 70 *Halibut with Walnuts Pappy Claude* Page 76 *Gravlax* Page 87 *Grilled Salmon Danish Style* Page 89 *Red Snapper Baked Alaska* Page 95 *Red Snapper with Fennel and Dill* Page 96 *Tuna Sushi in Chive Cream Sauce* Page 107 *Madison Avenue Stuffed Clams* Page 112 *Soft-Shell Crabs in Two Blankets* Page 115

Sauvignon Blanc (California)	*Joel's Barbecued Maine Lobster Page 124* *Mussels Sailor Fashion Page 128* *Shellfish Omelet Côte Opale Page 132* *Ravioli of Scallops Page 138* *Shrimp with Sour Cream Blésoise Page 144* *Squid Colin Maillard Page 145* *Sea Urchins in a Spinach Nest Page 148* *Terrine of Black Bass and Asparagus Page 150*
Sparkling Wine (California)	*Blue Point Oysters and Clams with Great Herbs Page 135*
Zinfandel (California)	*John Dory in Red Wine Page 27* *Cold American Char Forestière Page 55* *Grilled Whiting and Savoy Cabbage Page 58* *Codfish with Shallots and Red Wine Page 66* *Grouper with Three Vegetables Page 71* *Sautéed Haddock Mme. Colette Page 72* *Macaroni, Fennel and Sardine Pie Page 156* *Swordfish Pie Ajaccienne Page 160*

Index